TASTING
COLORADO

Favorite Recipes from the Centennial State

by Michele Morris

foreword by Eliza Cross

*Chris and Kerry,
Enjoy the tasting!
Michele*

FARCOUNTRY
PRESS
Helena, Montana

❧ For My Family ❧

ISBN 10: 1-56037-539-6
ISBN 13: 978-1-56037-539-5

© 2013 by Farcountry Press
Food photography and text © 2013 by Michele Morris
Colorado scenic photography © 2013 by Janine Fugere

For more information on our books, write Farcountry Press, P.O. Box 5630,
Helena, MT 59604; call (800) 821-3874; or visit www.farcountrypress.com.

Library of Congress Cataloging-in-Publication Data

Morris, Michele.
  Tasting Colorado : favorite recipes from the centennial state / by
Michele Morris.
      p. cm.
  Includes index.
  ISBN 978-1-56037-539-5
1. Cooking. 2. Cooking—Colorado. I. Title.
  TX714.M6775 2013
  641.59788--dc23
                              2012018012

Created, produced, and designed in the United States.
Printed in China.

17   16   15   14   13   1   2   3   4   5

contents

Acknowledgments ❧ xi

Foreword ❧ xiii

Introduction ❧ xvi

Guidelines for Recipes ❧ xviii

chapter 1: Breakfast & Brunch

Amish Breakfast Casserole ❧ 3

Blueberry Cake Muffins ❧ 4

Blueberry French Toast Strata ❧ 5

Cowboy Corn Cakes ❧ 6

Crème Brûlée French Toast ❧ 8

Dutch Apple Pancake ❧ 9

Eggnog Muffins ❧ 10

Granola ❧ 11

Ham and Portobello Mushroom Casserole ❧ 12

Lemon Poppy Seed Bread ❧ 13

Melon Ambrosia ❧ 14

North Fork Rabbit Hash with Poached Eggs ❧ 15

Oatmeal Nut Waffles ❧ 17

Orange, Cranberry, and Walnut Scones ❧ 18

Peach Bread ❧ 19

Sausage and Egg Casserole ❧ 20

Southwest Green Chile Toast ❧ 21

Swiss Chard and Gruyère Quiche ❧ 22

chapter 2: Appetizers & Snacks

Ajax Baked Chèvre ⁊ 24

Bear Creek Smoked Trout Pâté ⁊ 25

Broiled Pancetta-Wrapped Dates Stuffed with Gorgonzola ⁊ 26

Chile Crab Rolls with Charred Corn and Sriracha Mayo ⁊ 27

Chile Relleno of Crab ⁊ 28

Chipotle-Steeped Mussels ⁊ 30

Frico Caldo ⁊ 31

Goat Cheese Rosemary Biscuits ⁊ 33

Guacamole ⁊ 34

Herbed Spaetzle with Mushrooms and Braised Buffalo ⁊ 35

Mahi-Mahi Ceviche ⁊ 37

Pan-Fried Polenta with Grilled Pears and Gorgonzola Sauce ⁊ 38

Seared Scallops with Turnip Velouté, Celeriac, Apple, ⁊ 39
    and Fennel Salad, and Wild Boar Bacon Vinaigrette

Spicy Malted Lamb Ribs with Pistachio-Mint Recado ⁊ 41
    and Rose Blossom Yogurt

Sweet Potato Falafel with Lemon-Tahini Yogurt ⁊ 43

Tequila-Lime Salsa ⁊ 44

chapter 3: Salads & Sides

Baby Spinach and Bibb Lettuce Salad ⨯ 46
    with Chipotle-Buttermilk Dressing

Cauliflower and Summer Vegetables ⨯ 47

Crisp Gnocchi Salad with Wild Mushrooms and Asparagus ⨯ 48

Eggplant Caponata ⨯ 49

Farro and Barley "Risotto" ⨯ 50

The Fort's™ Famous Black Beans ⨯ 51

Frisée Salmon Salad ⨯ 52

Gingered Peas ⨯ 53

Grilled Palisade Peaches, Serrano Ham, and Rocket Salad ⨯ 55

Heirloom Tomato Salad with Fruition Farms Ricotta, ⨯ 56
    Eggplant Croutons, Arugula, and Romesco Vinaigrette

Lemon and Asparagus Risotto ⨯ 58

Mushroom and Brown Butter Risotto ⨯ 59

Olathe Sweet Corn Spoon Bread ⨯ 60

Poblano Chile and Chive Mashed Potatoes ⨯ 61

Portobello and Sage Bread Pudding ⨯ 62

Quinoa, Black Bean, and Corn Pilaf ⨯ 63

Sante Fe Chicken Salad ⨯ 64

Sautéed Brussels Sprouts with Chestnuts ⨯ 65

Spaghetti Squash Fritters ⨯ 67

Stone-Ground Bleu Cheese Grits ⨯ 68

Summer Caprese Salad ⨯ 70

Tomato and Watermelon Salad with Fennel Granita ⨯ 71

Tuscan Marinated Tomatoes ⨯ 72

Warm Goat Cheese Salad with Pistachios and Baby Beets ⨯ 73

Wedge Salad with Saison-Ranch Dressing ⨯ 74

chapter 4: Soups & Stews

Artichoke Bisque ❧ 77

Bison Chili ❧ 78

Buffalo Redeye Stew ❧ 79

Cream of Cilantro Soup ❧ 80

Curried Butternut Squash Soup ❧ 81

Gingery Cauliflower Soup ❧ 82

Green Chile Posole ❧ 83

Green Gazpacho ❧ 84

Lentil Soup with Prosciutto Chips ❧ 86

Smoked Pheasant Soup ❧ 87

Stracciatella ❧ 88

Sweet Corn Soup with Cilantro Puree ❧ 89

Tomato-Curry Soup ❧ 90

chapter 5: Main Courses

Alamosa Striped Bass ❧ 92

Braised Pork with Apples and Dijon ❧ 93

Chicken Stuffed with Mushrooms, Leeks, and Pistachios ❧ 94

Chile-Citrus Shrimp with Coconut Rice and ❧ 95
    Red Curry Vinaigrette

Chile-Seasoned Pot-Roasted Pork   97

Colorado Game Meatloaf   98

Colorado Leg of Lamb with Creamy Polenta and Lamb Jus   99

Elk Chops with Blackberry Sauce and Garlic Mashers   101

Espresso-Rubbed Beef Tenderloin   103

Fondue   104

Garlic and Sage–Stuffed Chicken Breasts   105

Grilled Shrimp with Tequila-Orange Sauce and Crispy   106
     Chorizo-Corn Relish

Jaeger Schnitzel with Wild Mushroom Sauce   108

Lamb Slider with Mint and Tomato-Ginger Chutney   109

Lobster Mac and Cheese   110

Mountain High Mac and Cheese   112

New York Strip Steaks with Gonzales Sauce   113

Pan-Roasted Colorado Striped Bass with Chanterelle   114
     Mushroom Vin Blanc

Peach BBQ Pork Spareribs   115

Portobello Mushroom Burger   116

Prosciutto-Wrapped Scallops with Fennel Gratin   117
     and Blood Orange Beurre Blanc

Raspberry-Chipotle Pork Tenderloin   119

Roast Colorado Lamb Chops with White Beans   120
     and Tarragon-Garlic Sauce

Salmon with Artichoke, Tomato, and Olive Tapenade   121

Slow-Poached Chicken with Red Pepper–Citrus Sauce   122
     and Stewed Artichoke

Southwestern Crab Cakes   125

Spaghetti with Braised Lamb Sugo   127

Spinach Florentine–Stuffed Trout   128

Tagliatelle Pasta with White Bolognese   129

Traditional Home-Style Red Chile Pork Tamales   130

Whiskey-Braised Lamb Shoulder   131

William Bent's Buffalo Tenderloin Filet Mignon   132

chapter 6: Desserts & Sweet Treats

Butterscotch and Banana Pudding   ∾   134

Carrot Cake   ∾   135

Chili-Chocolate Bourbon Cake   ∾   136

Chocolate-Cherry Mousse   ∾   138

Chocolate Chunk–White Chocolate Chip Cookies   ∾   140

Crisp Apple Tart   ∾   141

Espresso Ice Cream Cakes with White   ∾   142
     Chocolate-Blueberry Crust

Fruition Farms Ricotta Cheesecake   ∾   144

Fudge Brownies   ∾   145

Milk Stout Cupcakes   ∾   146

Pear Tart   ∾   147

Plum-Nectarine Crumble   ∾   148

Raspberry-Marsala Cake   ∾   149

Roasted Colorado Peach–Pistachio Brioche Pudding   ∾   150
     with Ice Cream

Valrhona Chocolate–Macadamia Nut Cake   ∾   152
     with Vanilla-Bourbon Anglaise

Yogurt Panna Cotta   ∾   153

Sources for Specialty Ingredients and Other Products   ∾   154

Contributors   ∾   155

Index   ∾   158

acknowledgments

I am grateful to several ambitious home cooks who volunteered their time to assist me in the kitchen during recipe testing and during photo shoots. They prepped food, held scrims and reflector cards, helped me select props, washed dishes, and, perhaps most importantly, kept me company. Thank you to Wendy Bermingham, Kathy Givan, her daughter Alexandra Givan, Kirsten Hall, Teresa Leede, Sharon Mehrtens, Mary Murray, Wendy Peterson, Michelle Pond, Florine Richardson, and her daughter Amy Richardson. I offer a special thanks to my daughter, Jenny Morris. Her own love of food, cooking, food styling, food photography, and blogging are a special thrill for me, her ideas and critiques during this process were invaluable, and she even shared her fabulous salsa recipe with me for the book.

I want to thank the staff at Farcountry Press. Jessica Solberg took a risk on hiring me to write my first cookbook, and her confidence was inspiring. Kathy Springmeyer, Shirley Machonis, Ann Seifert, and Will Harmon all provided wonderful insight and support, and their encouragement kept me motivated throughout the editing, design, and layout of the book. I especially appreciate that Farcountry Press gave me the opportunity to style the food and shoot my own photographs for the book.

My colleague Eliza Cross, who wrote the foreword for this book, helped me get started in the food-writing business. I've appreciated her support over the years, and I'm especially thankful to her for thinking enough of my work to refer Farcountry Press to me.

I need to thank my blog readers for waiting patiently during the six months of this project when I had little time to offer up new recipes and content because the cookbook was all consuming.

Special thanks are due to my close friends and family; they listened attentively while I talked about my project, they came to parties to eat the food I had prepared, and they offered endless encouragement.

I am proud to share this project with my sister, Janine Fugere, who provided the amazing Colorado scenic photography for the book. Her creativity and skill never cease to impress me, and I'm thankful she wanted to work together on the book.

Huge thanks are due to all the chefs who participated in this project. Their talent, creativity, and willingness to share were inspiring. I'm appreciative both of their recipes and their friendship.

Finally, I owe a very special thank you to my husband, Greg. He was happy to try every dish I put in front of him, even when all he wanted was a simple burger. He filled in as a hand model in photographs when I couldn't do it myself, and he waited patiently for me to transform the temporary test kitchen and photo studio back into our home. Above all, his support allows me to pursue my passion in the food world, and I'm eternally grateful for that.

foreword

by Eliza Cross

Does Colorado have a trademark food? It's a puzzle I've long pondered, especially when I learned that acclaimed food writer Michele Morris was compiling a cookbook. After all, Idaho has its potatoes, Maryland has its crab cakes, and Cheeseheads are proud to call Wisconsin home. Cities are known for their own characteristic fare, too, from Boston baked beans and Buffalo wings to Chicago deep-dish pizza and Philly cheesesteaks. So what about our state? Do we have a local food that truly embodies the Centennial State?

It's not a simple question to answer, given the unique geography and population of Colorado. Denver boasts a bustling culinary scene, with a recent surge of new restaurants featuring some of the country's top chefs and cuisine that is garnering national awards. Eateries for every appetite abound in Colorado's capital city—steak houses, sushi bars, barbecue joints, brasseries, pizzerias, brewpubs, delis, food trucks, cafés, bakeries, noodle shops, hot dog carts, and an array of ethnic eateries that rivals any large city.

Organic, locally sourced, sustainable ingredients may be all the rage, but Boulder residents—both the old-timers and the transplants—will tell you that good, healthful food has always been their fare of choice. The upscale resort towns of Aspen and Vail attract celebrity chefs like Nobu Matsuhisa and Wolfgang Puck, while the verdant Western Slope is home to wineries, fruit orchards, and produce growers. Ranchers on our eastern plains raise some of the country's best beef, lamb, and buffalo, and Colorado's mountain streams are swimming with freshwater fish like rainbow trout and coho salmon.

With such a dazzling variety of culinary choices in Colorado, how could we possibly choose just one to represent our fine state? For perspective on this appetizing conundrum, I turned to some of Colorado's most notable food lovers.

"Ever since I started writing about food in the late 1970s, I've been seeking the answer to this question," says *Aurora Sentinel* food columnist John Lehndorff, former dining critic for the *Rocky Mountain News* and author of *Denver Dines: A Restaurant Guide and More.* "Rocky Mountain oysters have been suggested repeatedly–but mainly by people who haven't tasted them. Boulder has been labeled the Silicon Valley of natural foods, but granola, tofu, and radish sprouts do not make for iconic state foods. Colorado is ground zero for the craft-brew revolution, so I guess Fat Tire is the state's trademark beverage. Based on sheer national impact and recognition, Colorado's iconic dish would have to be a foil-wrapped burrito or a bowl of macaroni and cheese; our state is the epicenter of fast, casual cuisine–home to Chipotle, Noodles & Company, Smashburger, and a host of national chains. Ultimately, though, Colorado has a buzz for culinary integrity and innovation created by acclaimed chefs, cheesemakers, salumi makers, ranchers, chocolatiers, mixologists, organic farmers, locavore activists, winemakers, brewers, mead makers, beekeepers, distillers, and retailers."

"No single dish can possibly capture the spirit of Colorado," says Shari Caudron, restaurant critic for *5280* magazine. "Instead, it's the way we eat that sets us apart. Whether it's a juicy bison rib-eye rubbed with smoked sea salt and extra virgin olive oil and grilled over a campfire, or a sweet sliced farmers' market tomato topped with tangy goat cheese and bright micro-greens, we eat the way we live–with energy, enthusiasm, respect for the environment, and extraordinary gratitude for the gifts that come from living here."

"Colorado is a hungry state," asserts Tucker Shaw, features and entertainment editor (and former food editor) of the *Denver Post.* "We're at the literal and virtual nexus of American culinary culture. Part of that is due to where we are on the map, but more of it is due to who we are and where we (and our parents) come from–which is everywhere. We revere what

grows in our own soil, from potatoes to lamb to wine, but we are also an itinerant group, intent on visiting the countries of the world and bringing the best back to inform our cooking. Do we have a trademark dish? Maybe not. But if we did, it would be dynamic: comforting, adventurous, surprising, mellow, and spicy all at once."

Finally, Tom "Dr. Colorado" Noel provides a bit of historical perspective: "Denver's Humpty Dumpty Drive-In claims to have invented the cheeseburger, and Baur's Restaurant is credited with inventing the ice cream soda—as a hangover cure," he says. "Other delicacies include the Denver omelet (add diced ham, onions, and peppers) and Rocky Mountain oysters, but probably the most memorable meal of all was Alfred Packer's feasting on five of his fellow prospectors as a blizzard blasted the San Juan Mountains."

So there you have it. Colorado cuisine may defy easy definition, but fortunately Michele Morris has traveled the state extensively to cull the most representative and delectable offerings. From the mountains to the valleys, from the small towns to the city streets, from the ski resorts to the back alleys and beyond, she's curated a compelling collection of quintessentially Colorado recipes and photos—guaranteed to give every reader a taste of our state's best.

Eliza Cross has written widely about Colorado cuisine and is the author of five books. She lives with her family in Centennial.

introduction

I settled in Colorado as a young bride in 1985, much like many who came here before me, enamored with the mountains and the scenery, eager to experience a bit of the Old West, and ready to set up my own homestead of sorts in the suburbs of Denver. Although Colorado natives, as well as longstanding residents of the state like me, might take offense to Denver being called "a cow town," the reality in 1985 was that Colorado, even Denver and the Front Range, lacked the breadth of dining options found in larger coastal cities like New York and San Francisco.

Today you'll find in Colorado one of the most exciting food scenes in the country. Classics like the Flagstaff House in Boulder are still going strong after forty years, but across the Front Range and scattered throughout the mountain towns is a proliferation of creative new culinary destinations. You can still experience the Old West at a guest dude ranch here, but chances are you'll be treated to some pretty upscale cuisine following your trail ride. Colorado's mountain resorts, offering some of the best skiing in the world, still lure skiers to their slopes for a day of fun in the snow and sun, but instead of simple cafeteria food for lunch, they now offer a Mobile Four Star restaurant on top of the mountain.

Here in Colorado, however, it's not just about world-class cuisine; Coloradans also care deeply about where their food comes from. And when it comes to locally grown food, Colorado is foodie heaven. In this book you'll find chefs who have forged strong ties with local farmers and restaurants, and tout those relationships on their menus, citing their sources for produce and livestock that eventually make their way onto the restaurants' ever-changing seasonal menus. In towns such as Boulder and Aspen, elaborate farm dinners in the field happen right down the street from restaurants offering fine dining on tables draped in white linen. Restaurants and diners alike seek organic foods, and eateries such as The Kitchen in Boulder have expanded recycling to a new level.

Many of our chefs have taken their relationship with their food sources a step further, launching their own farm operations and building a synergistic relationship between the farm and the restaurant. At Fruition in Denver, pork, lamb, and vegetables from the Fruition Farm show up on the menu, while food scraps from the restaurant make their way to the pig feed and compost piles on the farm. Chef and owner Alex Seidel thinks the symbiotic relationship is so important that all employees from the restaurant also work on the farm each week.

What has also changed over time in Colorado is the variety and breadth of food served in our constantly growing restaurant scene. You can still get a great steak in Colorado, and restaurants like The Fort™ and The Buckhorn Exchange are still popular for bison and game. But alongside these classics you can now find world-class Italian food at places like Frasca and Panzano, innovative Latin-influenced food brought to you by chefs like Richard Sandoval, incredibly creative fusion cuisine from restaurants like ChoLon, and a huge selection of inspired, delicious food from any number of our chefs and restaurants across the state.

It's not only the food being served here that makes the Colorado dining experience special. With nearly 100 vineyards and 80 wineries, our growing wine industry is gaining traction, winning awards, and producing some world-class wines that you'll also see on menus across the state. Our sommeliers, including nine Master Sommeliers, build impressive wine lists to pair with the food that you'll enjoy at these top restaurants. And if wine isn't your thing, you just might be interested to know that Colorado is home to one of the largest concentrations of craft brewing in our country and hosts the Great American Beer Festival each year. You'll even find recipes in this book that feature beers from some of these breweries.

Over the years, I grew tired of reading lists of so-deemed "top restaurants" or "best chefs" across the country and never seeing any names from Colorado. That's just not the case today. Our chefs are gaining reputations not only at home in Colorado, but across the food industry. And those of us who live here–or those of you who visit–are the lucky ones who get to experience their exciting food.

As I worked my way around the state to meet with chefs for this book, I was consistently struck by how open they were to sharing. Each one was generous and kind in working with me to craft recipes from their restaurants that home cooks can re-create. I had the pleasure of cooking, testing, and photographing each of these recipes myself, so I can attest firsthand to the deliciousness that is captured in this book. From the simplest muffin served at one of our cozy bed-and-breakfasts to the most decadent dish in the book–the Lobster Mac and Cheese–our chefs have served up an exciting collection of recipes. I am pleased and excited to share this cookbook with you. I hope you'll have as much fun preparing and sharing these delectable dishes as I did.

guidelines for recipes

Equipment:

- ✎ Oven temperatures are listed in degrees Fahrenheit.

- ✎ When a recipe calls for something to be pureed, you may either use an immersion stick blender or a traditional blender, but keep in mind that stick blenders generally don't produce a puree that is as smooth as a traditional blender. Many restaurant chefs strain pureed soups before serving them for a velvety smooth texture. You may do this if you wish, but it's not necessary in most cases, and this step is listed as optional in most recipes.

- ✎ When a recipe calls for adding ingredients to a pan or skillet over a certain heat level, you should heat the pan first, then add the ingredients to cook.

Adjusting Recipes for Lower Altitudes:

Recipes were tested at altitudes of 5,000 feet and higher. To use these recipes at lower altitudes, reduce oven temperatures by 25 degrees and increase leavening ingredients in baked goods. Some foods (like rice) may cook more quickly.

Ingredients and Preparation:

Most recipes specify either canola oil or extra virgin olive oil for cooking, and usually extra virgin olive oil as a finishing oil. You may substitute another vegetable oil for cooking if desired.

Fresh herbs enhance both the taste and the presentation of food and are called for in many of the recipes. Consider keeping an herb garden during the summer and potted herbs in your kitchen in the winter. Most grocery stores sell packaged fresh herbs year-round.

Unless otherwise stated, all-purpose flour should be used in any recipes calling for flour. If a recipe calls for cake flour, you may substitute 1 cup of all-purpose flour, less 2 tablespoons, mixed with 2 tablespoons cornstarch. To make self-rising flour, add a heaping teaspoon of baking powder plus ⅓ teaspoon of salt to 1 cup all-purpose flour.

A number of recipes include chile peppers or chili powder in the ingredients. Because the intensity of chiles and chili powder can vary greatly, as can individual sensitivity to the heat, taste your chiles first to determine how much heat they will add. If uncertain, start with a smaller amount than the recipe calls for and add more after tasting.

You'll find many recipes use heavy cream in the restaurant version of the recipe. For most soups and side dishes, you can substitute half-and-half or milk to reduce calories and fat, although the finished dish will not have the same rich flavor. In sauces where the cream is used to thicken a sauce or in baked goods, substitution is not recommended.

Several recipes call for roasted garlic. To quickly roast a large batch of garlic, place peeled cloves in a small saucepan and cover with extra virgin olive oil. Bring just barely to a simmer and cook until cloves are soft and take on a light golden-brown color, about an hour. Store unused roasted garlic along with the garlic-infused oil (which may also be used in recipes) in a covered container in the refrigerator.

Several recipes call for pureed chipotle chiles. To prepare the puree, rinse canned chipotle peppers in adobo sauce under water, then add to a blender along with enough water to process until smooth. Strain through a fine-mesh strainer and discard solids. Chipotle puree may be kept in a covered container in the freezer until needed, so it's usually easier to make a larger batch than you need for one recipe.

- *Butter* refers to salted whole butter unless noted otherwise.

- *Bread crumbs* refers to finely ground, dry, unseasoned bread crumbs unless noted otherwise.

- *Pepper* refers to ground black pepper unless noted otherwise.

- *Sugar* refers to granulated sugar unless noted otherwise. Brown sugar refers to light brown sugar.

When a recipe calls for stock (chicken, beef, or veal), you may substitute broth.

Nuts may be toasted either in the oven or on the stove. In the oven, spread nuts in a single layer on a baking sheet and bake at 350 degrees until lightly browned and aromatic. On the stove, spread nuts in a single layer in a skillet and cook over medium heat, stirring frequently, until nuts begin to brown and become aromatic. Nuts can burn very quickly once they start browning, so watch closely and do not overcook.

To roast peppers or chiles, place either whole chiles or flat pieces of peppers skin side down on a hot grill or skin side up under the broiler. Cook until the skin is completely blackened, then place in a covered container to steam until slightly cooled. Peel off the blackened skin and discard it, reserving the roasted peppers or chiles for the recipe. Unused roasted peppers and chiles may be stored in plastic bags in the freezer for up to six months.

Servings:

Some recipes produce more servings than a typical family would eat in one meal; recipes are noted if the leftovers freeze well.

Breakfast & Brunch

Orange, Cranberry, and Walnut Scones, p. 18

1 pound sliced bacon, diced

1 medium sweet onion, diced

6 eggs, lightly beaten

4 cups frozen shredded
   hash brown potatoes

2 cups shredded mild
   cheddar cheese

1 pound small-curd cottage cheese

1¼ cups shredded Swiss cheese

Makes 8 to 10 servings

Amish Breakfast Casserole

EASTHOLME IN THE ROCKIES B&B, CASCADE
INNKEEPER/OWNER DEBORAH RICE

This rich breakfast casserole, loaded with cheese, bacon, and potatoes, is irresistible.

Preheat the oven to 350 degrees. Spray a 13 x 9 x 2-inch glass baking dish with cooking spray.

Heat a large skillet over medium–high heat. Cook the bacon and onion together until bacon is crisp; drain fat. Combine the eggs, potatoes, cheddar cheese, cottage cheese, and Swiss cheese in a large bowl; add the bacon mixture and stir until well mixed.

Transfer to the prepared baking dish and bake, uncovered, until eggs are set and edges are lightly browned, about 40 minutes. Let stand 10 minutes before serving.

4 cups yellow cake mix

½ cup flour

2¼ cup rolled oats, divided

1¼ cup water

1 large egg

3 tablespoons canola oil

3 cups fresh or frozen blueberries

¼ cup flour

1 cup brown sugar

1 teaspoon cinnamon

1 teaspoon baking soda

6 tablespoons butter, melted

Yields 2 dozen muffins

Blueberry Cake Muffins

OLD TOWN GUESTHOUSE, COLORADO SPRINGS
SHIRLEY WICK

Bed and Breakfast Innkeepers of Colorado honored Shirley with a first place ribbon for these wonderfully sweet blueberry muffins.

Preheat the oven to 350 degrees. Line muffin tins with paper baking cups and spray with cooking spray.

Combine the dry cake mix, flour, and ¾ cup of the oats in a large bowl and stir until well mixed. Combine the water, egg, and oil in a small bowl and whisk to combine. Pour the wet ingredients into the cake mixture and stir until combined. Gently stir in the blueberries and divide batter between 24 baking cups.

To make the muffin topping, stir together the remaining 1½ cups of oats, flour, brown sugar, cinnamon, and baking soda; use a fork to mix in melted butter. Cover each muffin with some of the topping and lightly press the topping into the wet batter.

Bake until a toothpick inserted in the center comes out clean, about 30 to 35 minutes. Muffins freeze well and may be thawed at room temperature or gently in the microwave.

Blueberry French Toast Strata

THE BRADLEY BOULDER INN, BOULDER   KATIE COBLE

At this charming boutique hotel located just steps off Boulder's famous Pearl Street Mall, guests are treated to this sumptuous breakfast casserole. Raspberries may be substituted for the blueberries if desired.

12 slices white bread,
   crusts removed

8 ounces cream cheese,
   softened and cubed

1 cup fresh or frozen blueberries

10 large eggs

2 cups milk

1 teaspoon vanilla extract

½ teaspoon cinnamon

¼ teaspoon nutmeg

Makes 8 to 10 servings

Spray a 13 x 9 x 2-inch glass baking dish with cooking spray. Lay half of the bread slices over the bottom of the dish and distribute cubed cream cheese evenly over the top. Layer half of the blueberries over the cream cheese. Cover with remaining bread slices and top with remaining blueberries.

Whisk together the eggs, milk, vanilla, cinnamon, and nutmeg. Pour the egg mixture slowly over the bread, making sure that all the bread is moistened. Spray aluminum foil with cooking spray (to prevent sticking), cover, and refrigerate overnight.

Preheat the oven to 350 degrees. Bake for 1 hour; remove foil and place under the broiler briefly to lightly brown the top. Serve with maple syrup.

4 eggs

1 cup milk

2 tablespoons butter, melted

1 cup flour

¼ cup cornmeal

1 tablespoon baking powder

½ teaspoon salt

¼ teaspoon cayenne
pepper (optional)

3 cups fresh or frozen
sweet corn kernels

1 cup green chiles, chopped
(see Note)

Maple syrup

Makes 6 servings

Cowboy Corn Cakes

ROMANTIC RIVERSONG INN, ESTES PARK
OWNER GARY MANSFIELD

*The lodge now known as Romantic RiverSong Inn was originally built
as a summer retreat for a banking family from Kansas. Guests of the
inn today are treated to these unusual pancakes for breakfast.*

Beat the eggs and milk until blended; stir in butter. Combine the flour,
cornmeal, baking powder, salt, and cayenne and slowly stir into the
wet ingredients. Fold in corn and green chiles.

Using a ladle or an ice cream scoop, spoon the batter onto a greased
griddle or skillet over medium heat. Cook on the first side until
bubbles appear on top, and then flip and finish cooking on the
second side. Serve with maple syrup.

☙ **Note:** *The heat of green chiles can vary greatly, as can individual tolerance
for heat. If your chiles are medium or hot, or if you prefer a milder corn cake,
omit the cayenne.*

1 cup brown sugar

½ cup (1 stick) butter

2 tablespoons light corn syrup

8 slices French bread, 1 inch thick

1 ½ cups half-and-half

5 large eggs

1 teaspoon vanilla extract

1 tablespoon Grand Marnier

¼ teaspoon salt

Makes 8 servings

Crème Brûlée French Toast

THE CAPITOL HILL MANSION, DENVER   ❧   CARL SCHMIDT

Carl makes this sweet and filling French toast—which is rich enough to stand in as dessert—using farm fresh Colorado free-range eggs.

Heat the brown sugar, butter, and corn syrup in a saucepan, stirring frequently until blended and the sugar has melted. Pour the brown sugar mixture into a 13 x 9 x 2-inch glass baking dish and spread evenly over the bottom. Arrange the bread slices in a single layer over the brown sugar mixture.

Whisk the half-and-half, eggs, vanilla, Grand Marnier, and salt in a bowl until blended. Pour the mixture over the bread. Cover and refrigerate overnight.

Remove from the refrigerator and let the mixture stand at room temperature for 30 minutes. Preheat the oven to 350 degrees. Bake, uncovered, until puffed and golden brown, about 35 to 40 minutes. Serve immediately.

Dutch Apple Pancake

THE RUBY OF CRESTED BUTTE, CRESTED BUTTE
OWNERS CHEF CHRIS GREENE AND ANDREA GREENE

This recipe, with its beautiful presentation and aromatic baked apple and cinnamon flavors, is a favorite of guests at The Ruby. The apples can be prepared the night before and stored in an airtight container in the refrigerator.

5 large eggs

2 teaspoons vanilla extract

½ cup sugar

⅓ cup flour

1 teaspoon baking powder

Pinch sea salt

1½ tablespoons unsalted butter

2 large tart apples, peeled,
    cored, and cut into wedges
    ½ inch thick

1 teaspoon ground cinnamon

1 tablespoon sugar

Crème fraîche, for garnish
    (optional)

1 tablespoon powdered sugar,
    for garnish (optional)

Makes 4 to 6 servings

Preheat the oven to 375 degrees. Combine the eggs, vanilla, and ½ cup sugar in a blender and blend until combined, about 5 seconds. Add the flour, baking powder, and sea salt and mix until smooth, about 10 seconds longer.

Heat a 10-inch, oven-safe, nonstick skillet over medium heat and add the butter. When the butter has melted and the foam has subsided, add the apples and sauté, stirring occasionally, until softened, 4 to 5 minutes. Sprinkle the apples with the cinnamon and 1 tablespoon sugar; stir until well mixed. Sauté until the apples are glazed and the edges are slightly translucent, about 2 minutes longer.

Spread the apples evenly in the skillet and pour the batter slowly over the top so the apples stay in place. Reduce the heat to medium-low and cook until the bottom and sides start to firm up, about 8 minutes.

Transfer the pan to the oven and cook until the top of the pancake is firm and golden brown, about 10 minutes longer.

Remove from the oven and, after ensuring the sides are not sticking to the pan, invert a flat serving plate over the skillet. Holding the pan and plate together, turn both back over together and lift the pan off. Cut the pancake into six or eight wedges and transfer to individual plates. Top each portion with crème fraîche and sprinkle with powdered sugar.

1 large egg

⅓ cup canola oil

¾ cup eggnog

¾ cup rum

2 cups flour

1 tablespoon baking powder

½ teaspoon salt

⅔ cup sugar

1 teaspoon nutmeg

Yields 36 mini-muffins

Eggnog Muffins

CASTLE MARNE BED AND BREAKFAST, DENVER
MELISSA FEHER-PEIKER

The famous mansion housing Castle Marne Bed and Breakfast today was built in 1889 and designed by eclectic architect William Lang, perhaps best known as the creator of the Unsinkable Molly Brown House.

Preheat the oven to 350 degrees. Combine the egg, oil, eggnog, and rum in a small bowl and mix well; set aside.

Sift together the flour, baking powder, salt, and sugar in a large bowl. Make a well in the center of the dry ingredients and add the egg mixture, stirring just until the dry ingredients are moistened.

Spray mini-muffin pans with nonstick cooking spray and divide the batter evenly between 36 muffin cups, filling each about three-quarters full. Sprinkle the tops with nutmeg and bake until the tops are lightly browned, about 15 to 20 minutes.

❧ **Note:** *If you enjoy fresh-baked muffins every morning, the unbaked batter keeps very well for several days in an airtight container in the refrigerator.*

5 cups rolled oats

1 cup shredded coconut

½ cup sunflower seeds

¾ cup cashews

¾ cup walnut or pecan pieces

¼ cup sesame seeds

½ cup plus 2 tablespoons
    canola oil

½ cup plus 2 tablespoons honey

½ cup water

2 teaspoons vanilla extract

½ cup raisins

½ cup dried cranberries

Yields 12 cups

Granola

BRIAR ROSE BED & BREAKFAST, BOULDER ❧ JESSIKA HARDIN

Typical of health-conscious Boulder, the Briar Rose offers a vegetarian- and vegan-friendly menu to their guests, including this granola that they make exclusively from organic ingredients.

Preheat the oven to 325 degrees. Combine oats, coconut, sunflower seeds, cashews, walnuts, and sesame seeds in a large bowl and stir to mix. Combine oil, honey, water, and vanilla in a small bowl and whisk together. Pour wet mixture over dry ingredients and mix until completely coated.

Spread mixture on two greased baking sheets. Bake until golden brown, about 30 minutes, stirring every 10 minutes to ensure even browning. Remove from oven and let cool. Add raisins and cranberries, stir until well combined, and store in an airtight container.

Ham and Portobello Mushroom Casserole

LOS ALTOS BED & BREAKFAST, GRAND JUNCTION
OWNER YOUNG-JA GARRETT

Set in the expansive Grand Valley, with views of the magnificent Grand Mesa and Colorado National Monument, Los Altos Bed & Breakfast makes a perfect base from which to explore Colorado's wine country.

Preheat the oven to 350 degrees. Heat the oil in a medium skillet over medium-high heat; add the chopped mushrooms and sauté until softened and moisture is released, about 5 minutes.

Combine the ham, sour cream, onion, and mustard in a medium bowl and mix until smooth. Add the eggs, salt, and pepper and stir together. Add cheese and Portobello mushrooms and stir until combined.

Spray an 8 x 8 x 2-inch glass baking dish (or six individual ramekins) with cooking spray and pour in egg mixture. Bake until eggs are set, about 45 minutes for an 8 x 8 x 2-inch baking dish, or slightly less for individual ramekins.

1 tablespoon canola oil

1 medium Portobello mushroom cap, chopped

2 cups diced cooked ham

1 cup sour cream

2 tablespoons minced onion

2 teaspoons Dijon-style mustard

9 eggs, lightly beaten

½ teaspoon salt

¼ teaspoon pepper

¾ cup shredded sharp cheddar cheese

Makes 6 servings

3 cups flour

1 ⅓ cups sugar

1 teaspoon baking powder

1 ½ teaspoons salt

2 tablespoons poppy seeds

1 ¾ cups milk

1 cup canola oil

3 large eggs

1 ½ teaspoons lemon extract

1 ½ teaspoons butter extract
(optional)

Yields 1 loaf

Lemon Poppy Seed Bread

EASTHOLME IN THE ROCKIES B&B, CASCADE
INNKEEPER/OWNER DEBORAH RICE

*Listed on the National Register of Historic Places and nestled in the
foothills, with breathtaking views of Pikes Peak, this bed and breakfast
has been recognized repeatedly as one of the best in the West.*

Preheat oven to 350 degrees. Grease and flour a 9 x 5 x 3-inch
loaf pan.

Combine all ingredients together in a large mixing bowl and beat
with an electric mixer on medium for 1 to 2 minutes. Pour into
prepared loaf pan. Bake for 60 minutes. Cool on a wire rack and
remove from pan when cool.

2/3 cup freshly squeezed lime juice

1/4 cup sugar

1/4 cup honey

Chopped fresh mint

Ground ginger

2 cups balled or cubed watermelon

2 cups balled or cubed cantaloupe

2 cups balled or cubed honeydew

1/2 cup flaked coconut, toasted

Makes 8 servings

Melon Ambrosia

ROMANTIC RIVERSONG INN, ESTES PARK
OWNER GARY MANSFIELD

The combination of lime, mint, and ginger in this breakfast fruit salad turns everyday melon into a special treat.

Mix together the lime juice, sugar, and honey in a small bowl. Add chopped mint and ground ginger to taste and stir together.

Place the melon in a large mixing bowl and pour the lime mixture over the melon. Toss gently, making sure to coat evenly. When serving, sprinkle with toasted coconut.

2 ounces dry porcini mushrooms

1 ½ cups dry Marsala

4 rabbit legs, bone in and
    trimmed of fat (or chicken thighs)

Salt and pepper

Flour, for dredging

1 tablespoon extra virgin olive oil

½ cup diced pancetta

½ white onion, finely diced

2 tablespoons minced garlic

1 tablespoon tomato paste

1 (14-ounce) can chicken stock

1 small bay leaf

2 cups diced fingerling potatoes,
    roasted

2 cups seeded and coarsely
    chopped heirloom tomatoes

2 cups greens (beet tops, radish
    tops, or spinach)

6 soft-poached eggs

Grated Parmigiano-Reggiano
    cheese, for garnish

North Fork Rabbit Hash with Poached Eggs

THE PULLMAN, GLENWOOD SPRINGS   ❦   CHEF MARK FISCHER

The hearty hash served at The Pullman is made from rabbit legs and is equally good for breakfast, lunch, or dinner—substitute chicken thighs if you can't find rabbit or prefer chicken instead.

Preheat the oven to 300 degrees. Combine the porcini and Marsala in a small saucepan and bring to a simmer; turn off heat and let mushrooms steep.

Season rabbit with salt and pepper and dredge in flour, shaking off excess. Heat the olive oil in a medium skillet over medium-high heat and brown rabbit legs on both sides. Transfer to a small Dutch oven or roasting pan.

Discard all but a film of oil from the skillet. Add the pancetta and brown over medium heat. Add the onions and garlic and cook until soft and lightly brown. Add the tomato paste and cook, stirring until well incorporated. Add the chicken stock and bay leaf and stir until evenly mixed. Add the mushrooms and Marsala and stir together.

Pour the mixture over the rabbit, cover, and cook in the oven until rabbit meat easily falls from the bone, about 2 hours. Remove meat, cool, and shred by hand. Return shredded meat to the cooking liquid, remove the bay leaf, and season with salt and pepper to taste.

Combine rabbit with roasted potatoes and tomatoes and heat in the oven until evenly warmed. Stir in the greens to wilt. Divide hash evenly between six ramekins and top each with a poached egg. Garnish with grated cheese and serve immediately.

❦ **Note:** *The rabbit may be prepared the day before.*

Makes 6 servings

1 ½ cups whole wheat flour

2 teaspoons baking powder

½ teaspoon salt

2 cups milk

4 tablespoons butter, melted

2 eggs, well beaten

2 tablespoons honey

1 cup rolled oats

1 cup chopped walnuts

Maple syrup, for garnish

Whipped cream, for garnish

Makes 8 servings

Oatmeal Nut Waffles

HOLDEN HOUSE 1902 BED & BREAKFAST INN, COLORADO SPRINGS
SALLIE CLARK

Holden House has been honored with a Historic Preservation Alliance Award of Excellence for their historic preservation and restoration of the inn.

Sift together the whole wheat flour, baking powder, and salt. Add the milk, butter, eggs, and honey and stir to combine. Stir in oats and walnuts.

Preheat a waffle iron and spray with cooking spray. Pour batter onto the greased waffle iron, close, and cook until browned and cooked through, about 2 minutes. Repeat with remaining batter. Serve waffles with maple syrup and whipped cream.

❧ *Note: You may substitute ½ to 1 cup unsalted sunflower seeds for the walnuts if desired. Batter may also be used to make pancakes.*

½ cup dried cranberries

¼ cup orange juice

2¼ cups self-rising flour

¼ cup brown sugar

2 tablespoons powdered milk
   (dry milk)

4 tablespoons butter, cut into
   small cubes, chilled

½ cup chopped walnuts

1 small orange, zested

½ cup milk

1 egg

1 egg yolk, white reserved
   and lightly beaten

Yields 8 large scones

The main house of the historic
Hooper Homestead was built in
1878 and constructed entirely
of brick that was manufactured
on-site by owner Thomas Hooper
himself. Called "Hooper Brick," the
brick was instrumental in helping
to rebuild Central City after the
great fire of 1874.

Orange, Cranberry, and Walnut Scones

HOOPER HOMESTEAD, CENTRAL CITY　❧　CHRISTINE POLLOCK

Orange and cranberry marry beautifully in scones served at this historic 1880s Victorian-era inn in Central City, home to the Central City Opera House, whose summer festival attracts tourists from across the country.

Preheat the oven to 400 degrees. Line a baking sheet with parchment paper or a silicone baking mat. Soak the cranberries in the orange juice in a small bowl and set aside.

Add the flour, brown sugar, and powdered milk to a large bowl and stir together. Cut in the butter with a pastry cutter or your fingers. Stir in the walnuts and orange zest. Add the milk, whole egg, and egg yolk to the cranberries and beat lightly. Add the cranberry mixture to the flour mixture and stir lightly with a fork just until moistened.

Turn the dough onto a floured board and work briefly to pull dough together. Pat into a circle about 1 inch thick and cut into eight equal wedges.

Arrange the scones on the baking sheet, leaving about 1 inch between wedges, and brush tops with beaten egg white. Bake for 16 to 18 minutes. If top of scones are not browned, you may broil for 1 to 2 minutes to brown.

Remove scones from the oven and place on a wire rack until cool. Serve with butter and homemade jams or preserves.

(see photograph on page 1)

3 cups flour

1 teaspoon salt

½ teaspoon baking soda

1 teaspoon baking powder

1 tablespoon cinnamon

3 eggs

1 cup canola oil

2 cups sugar

2 cups chopped fresh or
    frozen peaches

1 tablespoon vanilla extract

1 cup chopped nuts

Yields 2 loaves

Peach Bread

LOS ALTOS BED & BREAKFAST, GRAND JUNCTION
OWNER YOUNG-JA GARRETT

Many Coloradans feel the peaches in Palisades are the best in the world, and guests at Los Altos, on the Western Slope, enjoy peach bread and homemade peach preserves daily.

Preheat the oven to 325 degrees. Grease two 9 x 5 x 3-inch loaf pans. Sift together the flour, salt, baking soda, baking powder, and cinnamon and set aside.

Beat the eggs in a large bowl using an electric mixer. Add the oil and sugar and beat well. Add the peaches and vanilla and mix briefly to combine. Add the sifted dry ingredients and mix well; stir in chopped nuts.

Spoon batter into prepared loaf pans and bake for 1 hour. Let cool slightly on a wire rack before removing from the pan.

1 pound ground breakfast sausage

½ pound shredded sharp cheddar
    cheese, divided

½ teaspoon dry mustard

½ teaspoon paprika

1 cup sour cream

1 teaspoon baking powder

½ cup flour

2 cups cottage cheese

1 teaspoon salt

16 large eggs

Makes 8 to 10 servings

Georgetown, a charming
nineteenth-century mining town
nestled in the mountains forty-five
miles west of Denver, has been
designated a National Historic
Landmark District and is known
as the Silver Queen of the Rockies.

Sausage and Egg Casserole

SILVER QUEEN BED & BREAKFAST, GEORGETOWN
OWNER JOYCE JAMELE

*Joyce's breakfast casserole is easy to assemble, can be made partially
in advance, and fills you up. It's a perfect start to a day of hiking
near Georgetown for guests of the bed and breakfast.*

Preheat the oven to 325 degrees. Heat a large skillet over medium-
high heat and brown sausage; drain excess fat.

Spray a 13 x 9 x 2-inch glass baking dish with cooking spray and
spread half the cheddar cheese evenly over the bottom of the dish.

Combine the dry mustard, paprika, and sour cream in a medium
bowl; stir in the sausage until well mixed. Spread the mixture over
cheese. Recipe can be prepared up to this point the night before,
covered, and stored in the refrigerator.

Stir the baking powder, flour, and cottage cheese together in a small
bowl. Combine the salt and the eggs in a large bowl and beat until
fluffy. Add the cottage cheese, stir the mixture together, and pour
over the cheddar cheese and sausage in the baking dish. Sprinkle
remaining cheddar cheese over the top. Bake, uncovered, until
eggs are set, about 45 minutes.

1 loaf crusty, rustic bread

¼ to ⅓ cup chopped fresh or
    frozen green chiles, to taste

1 pound guacamole

12 large eggs

½ cup milk

½ teaspoon salt

½ teaspoon pepper

½ teaspoon garlic powder

12 ounces shredded cheddar
    cheese, or more as needed
    to cover toast

Sour cream, for garnish

Salsa, for garnish

Chopped cilantro, for garnish

Makes 8 servings

Southwest Green Chile Toast

MARIPOSA LODGE, STEAMBOAT SPRINGS ❧ DANIELLE STEEVES

This rustic open-faced breakfast sandwich has unmistakable Southwestern flavors.

Slice off the ends of the loaf of bread and then slice the bread on the diagonal into eight pieces; discard the ends and toast bread slices; set aside. Mix the green chiles into the guacamole and set aside.

Combine the eggs, milk, salt, pepper, and garlic powder in a large bowl and beat together. Heat a large nonstick skillet over medium-high heat and scramble the eggs, stirring frequently, until just barely wet.

Spread the guacamole evenly over each slice of toast, top with scrambled eggs, and sprinkle on enough cheddar cheese to cover the eggs. Place on a baking sheet and broil for 1 to 2 minutes to melt cheese and lightly brown.

To serve, top with a dollop of sour cream and a sprinkle of chopped cilantro. Serve with salsa on the side.

2 tablespoons extra virgin olive oil

½ medium sweet onion, chopped

¾ cup chopped, cooked
   Swiss chard

1 garlic clove, minced

1 pie crust to fit a 9-inch
   deep-dish pie pan

1 cup shredded Gruyère cheese,
   2 tablespoons reserved

5 large eggs

1 cup whole milk

⅛ teaspoon hot sauce

½ teaspoon salt

¼ teaspoon pepper

⅛ teaspoon garlic powder,
   or to taste

Makes 4 to 6 servings

Swiss Chard and Gruyère Quiche

MARIPOSA LODGE, STEAMBOAT SPRINGS ❧ DANIELLE STEEVES

While the big draw in Steamboat is the snow, lovingly called Champagne Powder, the town is equally appealing in the summer. Guests at the lodge are treated to a gourmet breakfast before setting out to enjoy the town or the slopes.

Preheat the oven to 375 degrees. Heat the olive oil in a medium skillet over medium-high heat and add onion; cook until slightly softened, about 3 minutes. Add the Swiss chard and garlic and sauté for another 1 to 2 minutes.

Fit the pie crust into a 9-inch deep-dish pie pan and sprinkle the cheese evenly over the bottom of crust, reserving 2 tablespoons. Spread the Swiss chard mixture over the top of the cheese.

Combine the eggs, milk, hot sauce, salt, pepper, and garlic powder in a large bowl and beat together. Pour the egg mixture over the top of the Swiss chard mixture and sprinkle the reserved cheese over the top.

Bake, uncovered, until eggs are set and the top is a light golden brown, about 45 minutes.

Appetizers & Snacks

Chipotle-Steeped Mussels, p. 30

Chèvre

8 ounces Avalanche fresh chèvre or any local fresh goat's cheese

4 roasted garlic cloves, minced *(see Guidelines for Recipes on page xviii)*

6 oil-cured black olives, pitted and sliced

Pinch herbs de Provence

⅓ cup tomato sauce, recipe below, or use high-quality store-bought sauce

Toasted sourdough bread as accompaniment

Tomato sauce

2 tablespoons extra virgin olive oil

¼ cup sliced garlic

1 cup diced red onion

Pinch crushed red pepper flakes

1 (28-ounce) can of San Marzano tomatoes or other high-quality tomatoes

Salt and pepper

Makes 4 servings

Ajax Baked Chèvre

AJAX TAVERN AT THE LITTLE NELL, ASPEN
EXECUTIVE CHEF ALLISON JENKINS

This easy-to-make baked chèvre with flavors of pizza can be increased to any proportion and is equally great for crowds or a lunch for one.

For the chèvre:
Preheat the oven to 350 degrees. Press the goat cheese into a small baking dish, just large enough to fit the cheese with room for toppings. Top the cheese evenly with the roasted garlic, olives, herbs, and tomato sauce. Bake, uncovered, until hot and bubbly, about 10 minutes. Serve with toasted sourdough bread.

For the sauce:
Cook the garlic and onion over low heat in the extra virgin olive oil until translucent, making sure not to brown. Add a pinch crushed red pepper flakes and the tomatoes; simmer for 30 minutes. Season with salt and pepper to taste and puree with a food mill or food processor. Refrigerate extra sauce for up to 1 week or freeze for 6 months.

Bear Creek Smoked Trout Pâté

HIGHLAND HAVEN CREEKSIDE INN, EVERGREEN   ✤   GAIL RILEY

Bear Creek is a classic small stream in Colorado and a great place to fish for wild brook trout in a gorgeous setting. While there is public access to the headwaters, much of the creek around Evergreen is private. Virtually any smoked fish will work in this recipe if you can't find smoked trout.

12 ounces smoked trout meat, crumbled

1 cup cream cheese

1 cup cottage cheese

1 teaspoon prepared horseradish

1 teaspoon lemon juice

Pepper

1 tablespoon chopped fresh parsley

1 tablespoon bread crumbs

2 tablespoons capers

2 tablespoons diced red onion

Paprika, for garnish (optional)

Toast points, baguette slices, or crackers, for serving

Makes 8 to 10 servings

Place the fish, cream cheese, cottage cheese, horseradish, and lemon juice in a food processor or blender and mix until smooth. Season with pepper to taste; add the parsley and bread crumbs and blend well.

Line a fish–shaped mold with plastic wrap and spoon the trout pâté into the mold. Cover with plastic wrap, press firmly into the mold, and refrigerate for 8 hours.

Unmold onto a serving plate and garnish with capers and diced red onion. Lightly sprinkle with paprika for color, if desired. Serve with toast points, baguette slices, or crackers.

✤ **Note:** *If you don't have a mold, you can shape a fish by hand, using capers for the eyes, and create an impressive presentation on a platter of decorative lettuce. Alternatively, simply spoon the pâté into a bowl and serve.*

24 large Medjool dates,
  split and seeds removed

1 cup Gorgonzola cheese

24 very thin (2-inch-long) slices
  pancetta

Makes 12 servings

Broiled Pancetta-Wrapped Dates Stuffed with Gorgonzola

PANZANO, HOTEL MONACO, DENVER
EXECUTIVE CHEF ELISE WIGGINS

A simple yet elegant appetizer that's perfect for a large crowd.

Stuff the dates with Gorgonzola, wrap with pancetta slices, and secure with toothpicks so they won't unwrap while cooking. Broil until pancetta is crispy and lightly browned.

❧ **Note:** *If you are concerned about burning the pancetta on the broil setting, bake in a preheated oven at 400 degrees until done.*

Crab rolls

1 ounce cooked rice noodles or vermicelli noodles, tossed lightly with canola oil

2 ounces jumbo lump blue crab

1 green onion, thinly sliced

2 tablespoons sweet corn kernels, charred in a small skillet or wok

1 tablespoon roughly chopped cilantro

2 (8-inch) rice paper wraps

2 large red lettuce leaves

Pickled peppers, for garnish (optional)

Sriracha mayo

½ cup mayonnaise

1 tablespoon Sriracha chile sauce

1 tablespoon lime juice

Makes 2 servings

Chile Crab Rolls with Charred Corn and Sriracha Mayo

CHOLON MODERN ASIAN BISTRO, DENVER
CHEF LON SYMENSMA

Chef Lon Symensma attended the Culinary Institute of America and worked in Michelin-starred restaurants before settling down to open his own restaurant in Denver. His delicate and innovative Asian-fusion cuisine is a testament to how much the food scene in Colorado has evolved in recent years.

For the crab rolls:
Combine cooked noodles, crab, green onion, corn, and cilantro in a small bowl and stir together; set aside.

Run one rice paper wrap under warm water for about 10 seconds, then lay flat on a cutting board. Line the inside of the wrap with a red lettuce leaf, leaving about ½ inch around the edges of the wrap for folding over and sealing. Place half of the noodle mixture in a line down the center; fold the sides in and top over as if you are making an envelope, then roll, sealing the edges. Place seam side down on the cutting board. Repeat to fill the second wrap.

❧ **Note:** *Instead of making two smaller rolls, you may make one large roll by using all the filling in a single wrap and wrapping it again with the second rice paper wrap to hold it firmly together. Cut in half to create two servings.*

For the Sriracha mayo:
Combine all ingredients in a small bowl and stir until well mixed.

Presentation:
Slice crab rolls in half diagonally and serve with pickled peppers and Sriracha mayo.

Rellenos

6 mild chile peppers, 4 to 6 inches long (see Note)

1 tablespoon unsalted butter

1½ cups sweet corn kernels

¼ cup finely diced red bell pepper

¼ cup finely diced poblano pepper

1 to 2 tablespoons minced fresh ginger

4 ounces fresh jumbo lump blue crab

Lemon juice

Salt and pepper

Cilantro sprigs, for garnish (optional)

Carrot-ginger butter

½ cup white wine

¼ cup white vinegar

1 cup fresh carrot juice

1 tablespoon minced fresh ginger

1 shallot, chopped

1 bay leaf

½ cup heavy cream

4 tablespoons unsalted butter

Salt and pepper

Makes 6 servings

Chile Relleno of Crab

CARIBOU CLUB, ASPEN ❧ EXECUTIVE CHEF MILES ANGELO

These unusual crab rellenos, served with a tangy butter sauce, are garnished with vinegar black beans at the Caribou Club. The black bean recipe from The Fort™ on page 51 would work well.

For the rellenos:
Blister the skin of the chiles over an open flame, cover, and set aside. While chiles cool, heat a large skillet over high heat and add the butter to melt. Add the corn, cook until charred, then set aside.

Combine red pepper, poblano pepper, and ginger in a medium bowl; add corn and stir until well mixed. Gently fold in the crab, being careful not to break up the lumps; season with lemon juice, salt, and pepper to taste.

When chiles have cooled, peel off the charred skin and remove the seeds by making a small incision; be careful to keep the chile and stem intact. Stuff each chile with 2 to 3 tablespoons of the crab stuffing and wrap each relleno in plastic wrap.

Place a steamer rack or insert over simmering water. Place wrapped chiles into the steamer insert, cover, and steam until warm inside, about 8 to 10 minutes.

Spoon 2 tablespoons of the carrot-ginger butter onto six warm plates. Remove chiles from plastic wrap and place on top of the butter sauce. Garnish the plates with cilantro sprigs.

❧ **Note:** *The chef at the Caribou Club prefers mild lipstick chiles, which are small red chiles that are pointed at the end. These chiles can be difficult to find, but mild Anaheim chiles work equally well.*

For the carrot-ginger butter:

Combine white wine, vinegar, carrot juice, ginger, shallot, and bay leaf in a medium saucepan over medium-high heat; cook until almost dry.

Stir in the cream and cook until reduced by half. Lower heat and whisk in the butter. Strain through a fine-mesh strainer into a small bowl and discard solids; keep sauce warm until ready to use.

1 tablespoon extra virgin olive oil

2 pounds mussels, cleaned
    and beards removed

2 ounces minced garlic,
    about 10 cloves

2 ounces minced shallot,
    about 2 medium shallots

¼ cup white wine

¾ cup chicken stock

2 tablespoons capers

1 tablespoon chipotle puree
    (see Guidelines for Recipes on
    page xviii), more or less to taste

¾ cup marinara sauce

Freshly squeezed lemon juice,
    for garnish

Cilantro sprigs, for garnish

Grilled baguette slices

Extra virgin olive oil,
    for baguette slices

Makes 4 servings (2 entrée servings)

Chipotle-Steeped Mussels

ST. REGIS ASPEN RESORT, ASPEN
EXECUTIVE CHEF JASON ADAMS

*Be sure to have plenty of crusty baguette slices on hand for soaking up
all of the delicious chipotle sauce from the cooking liquid of the mussels.*

Heat the olive oil in a large skillet over medium–high heat. Add the
mussels, garlic, and shallots and sauté together for 2 minutes, stirring
frequently. Add the white wine, chicken stock, capers, chipotle puree,
and marinara sauce and stir together; simmer until mussels open,
about 3 to 5 minutes.

Place the mussels in a serving bowl, pour the sauce over, and garnish
with a squeeze of lemon juice and the cilantro sprigs. Serve with
grilled baguette slices that have been brushed with olive oil.

(see photograph on page 23)

Denver, the capital of Colorado, is known as the Mile High City because of its
elevation of 5,280 feet above sea level, which is marked by a golden dome on
the steps of the capitol. Unlike most cities, Denver was not built on a road, railroad, or navigable body of water when it was founded. Instead, the discovery
of gold here in 1858 seemed as good a reason as any for pioneers to lay down
roots. Three towns with different names once stood where Denver now stands,
but in 1859, a barrel of whiskey was shared by all when residents agreed to
drop the other names. It comes as no surprise then that the first permanent
structure in Denver was a saloon.

Frico

1 medium Yukon Gold potato
    (about 4 to 5 ounces)

1 teaspoon grape seed or canola oil

2 tablespoons minced onion

¼ cup grated hard Italian cheese,
    such as Montasio, Piave,
    or Parmigiano-Reggiano

Pinch salt

Grated nutmeg

4 pieces of thinly sliced prosciutto

Cilantro vinaigrette

1 tablespoon chopped fresh cilantro

1 tablespoon grape seed or
    canola oil

1 teaspoon minced shallot

Sherry vinegar

Salt

Makes 4 servings

Frico Caldo

FRASCA FOOD AND WINE, BOULDER
CHEF LACHLAN MACKINNON-PATTERSON

When Food & Wine *magazine named MacKinnon-Patterson one of America's Best New Chefs in 2005, the editors were impressed with his ability to do amazing things with the most basic ingredients. Indeed he does, as you'll find in these simple potato pancakes typical of the Friuli region of Italy.*

For the frico:
Simmer the unpeeled potato in a saucepan of salted water until fork tender, about 30 to 45 minutes. Drain, cool, and peel the potato, then crush into small pieces.

Heat a small sauté pan over medium heat, add the grape seed or canola oil and the onion; sauté until translucent, about 3 minutes. Combine the crushed potato with the onion, cheese, salt, and nutmeg to taste in a small bowl, taking care not to over-mix.

Heat a 6- to 8-inch nonstick skillet over medium-high heat. Spray lightly with cooking spray and add the potato mixture, pressing down gently to form a pancake. Cook on one side until golden brown, about 4 to 5 minutes. Use a spatula to flip and complete cooking for 4 to 5 minutes on the second side.

For the cilantro vinaigrette:
Mix together the cilantro, oil, and shallot. Whisk in vinegar and salt to taste.

Presentation:
Cut the frico into four wedges and top each with one piece of sliced prosciutto. Serve with cilantro vinaigrette.

*❧ **Note:** If you have trouble flipping the frico with a spatula, try inverting a plate over the top of the pan, then turning both over together; slide the frico back into the pan on the uncooked side to finish cooking.*

5 cups flour (plus more for dusting)

2 tablespoons baking powder

1 teaspoon kosher salt

¼ cup sugar

1½ tablespoons chopped
    fresh rosemary

¾ cup (1½ sticks) butter, diced,
    very cold

8 ounces goat cheese, crumbled
    small

1¼ cups buttermilk (plus more
    for brushing biscuits)

¾ cup whole milk

Sea salt, for sprinkling

Yields 14 large or 20 medium biscuits

Goat Cheese Rosemary Biscuits

JENNIFER JASINSKI, DENVER
EXECUTIVE CHEF AND OWNER OF RIOJA, BISTRO VENDOME,
AND EUCLID HALL

The creation of this delicious bread started with the idea that restaurant guests would appreciate a variety of bread styles and types to be served at the table. While the buttery, flaky biscuits are great served on their own, they can also be used as sandwich bread (the chef uses them for her lamb dip sandwich) or even as the muffin under an eggs Benedict.

Preheat the oven to 400 degrees. Mix together the flour, baking powder, salt, sugar, and rosemary in a large bowl. Add the diced butter to the bowl, rubbing it into the flour with your hands until the butter is pea-size. Do the same with the goat cheese. Add the buttermilk and milk all at once, mixing just until the dough comes together. Do not over-mix.

Turn the dough out onto a lightly floured surface and roll it out to a square about 1 inch thick. Make a three-way fold by folding the two outside edges together into the center (like a tri-fold on a letter), and then fold the piece of dough in half. Roll out again to 1 inch thick, repeat a three-fold of the dough, and then roll it out once again about 1 inch thick.

Use a 3-inch cutter (for large biscuits) to cut the biscuits. Line a baking sheet with parchment paper or a silicone baking liner. Place the cut biscuits on the pan, brush the dough with a bit of buttermilk, and sprinkle the top of each biscuit with sea salt.

Bake biscuits until puffed and golden brown, about 15 to 18 minutes. Depending on your oven, you may need to turn the tray once for even browning.

❧ *Note: Don't discard your scraps of dough; press them together and refrigerate or freeze them for another use. They won't rise quite as much when baked, but they'll still be delicious. To prepare ahead, you can make the dough and refrigerate it for up to one week or freeze it.*

5 whole Hass avocados

1 cup diced tomatoes

1 cup finely diced white onions

⅓ cup chopped fresh cilantro

1 teaspoon salt, or to taste

Makes 6 servings

Guacamole

TAMAYO, DENVER
EXECUTIVE CHEF RICHARD SANDOVAL
CHEF DE CUISINE ARNOLD RUBIO

Richard Sandoval has created a restaurant empire with top-rated restaurants across the world. Colorado is home to Zengo, Venga Venga, La Sandia, Cima, and Tamayo, where his Latin roots clearly influence the menu.

Cut the avocados in half and remove the pits and skin. Mash the avocados in a large bowl; add remaining ingredients and stir together. Adjust salt to taste.

Buffalo ribs

1 ½ pounds boneless buffalo short ribs (or about 2 pounds bone in)

1 ¾ cups flour, divided

2 tablespoons canola oil

2 large carrots, cut into thirds

2 celery stalks, cut into thirds

2 sweet onions, cut into quarters

8 garlic cloves, crushed

2 large sprigs fresh rosemary

1 small bunch fresh thyme sprigs

1 cup dry red wine

1 quart beef stock

Spaetzle

3 tablespoons salt

½ cup milk

1 cup fresh parsley leaves

1 egg

3 tablespoons water

Herbed Spaetzle with Mushrooms and Braised Buffalo

HOTEL JEROME, ASPEN ❧ EXECUTIVE CHEF RICH HINOJOSA

The Hotel Jerome uses shimeji mushrooms, when available, which have a long, tender stem and a small dark-brown button top, but you can substitute any mushroom you like in this wonderfully rich and savory dish. The short ribs and the spaetzle can be prepared the day before and then the dish assembled just before serving to save time. This hearty appetizer can also be served as an entrée.

For the buffalo ribs:
Preheat the oven to 275 degrees. Season the short ribs very generously with salt and pepper, then dust with ½ cup of the flour, shaking off the excess. Heat oil in a medium stockpot or Dutch oven and brown the ribs well on all sides; remove from pot and set aside.

Add the carrot, celery, and onion to the pot and cook until vegetables are lightly browned, about 5 minutes. Add the garlic, rosemary, and thyme and place the ribs back into the pot. Deglaze by adding the red wine and gently scraping the bottom of the pot with a wooden spoon to pull up all the browned bits. Pour in the beef stock and cover tightly.

Place the stockpot in the preheated oven and cook the ribs until the beef is falling apart, about 6 to 8 hours. Remove the beef and shred; set aside. Strain the broth through a fine-mesh strainer into a medium bowl, reserving the broth and discarding solids. The short ribs may be prepared a day ahead and refrigerated.

For the spaetzle:
Bring a large stockpot of water to a boil and add 3 tablespoons of salt to the water. Pour the milk into a small saucepan and bring just to a simmer; remove from heat.

(continued on page 36)

Mushrooms

Canola oil

1 teaspoon finely minced onion

8 ounces fresh shimeji or other
    seasonal mushrooms, cleaned
    (see Note)

½ cup (1 stick) unsalted butter,
    divided

¼ cup chicken stock

Salt and pepper

Makes 8 servings

Place the parsley in a blender and add about half of the scalded milk. Blend on medium until well combined, then slowly add the remaining milk and blend until very smooth.

Whisk the egg and water together in a medium bowl, then whisk in the green milk mixture. Add the remaining 1¼ cups of flour to a large bowl and pour the milk mixture into the flour, stirring until well blended. The batter should feel soft.

Working in small batches, spoon the batter through a spaetzle maker or large-holed colander into the pot of boiling water. When the pasta floats, scoop it out with a slotted spoon and place into a mixing bowl. Toss with a little canola oil so it doesn't stick together; set aside. Continue working in batches until you have cooked all the spaetzle. The spaetzle may be prepared the day before.

For the mushrooms:
Heat about a tablespoon of canola oil in a large skillet over medium-high heat; add the finely minced onions and cook until just translucent, about 1 minute. Add the mushrooms to the pan and sauté until lightly browned, about 20 minutes. Add 1 tablespoon of the butter and deglaze by adding the chicken stock and gently scraping the bottom of the pan. Season with salt and pepper to taste; simmer until the mushrooms are tender.

To assemble:
Heat a large nonstick sauté pan over medium-high heat and add the remaining butter. Toss the spaetzle in the butter until well coated, and allow to brown just slightly. Add the cooked mushrooms and the short rib meat, along with 1 cup of the reserved broth; bring to a simmer. Season with salt and pepper to taste. Divide the mixture among six pasta bowls and serve.

⁋ *Note: If using a thin mushroom such as shimeji or enoki, leave whole; if using a large mushroom such as a crimini or white button, thinly slice.*

8-ounce mahi-mahi fillet, diced

1½ tablespoons salt

1 cup freshly squeezed lime juice

6 tablespoons orange juice

6 tablespoons honey

½ cup ketchup

½ cup diced white onions

½ cup diced tomatoes

½ ounce chopped fresh cilantro
    (about ⅓ cup)

Buffalo-style classic hot sauce

Makes 4 servings

Mahi-Mahi Ceviche

TAMAYO, DENVER
EXECUTIVE CHEF RICHARD SANDOVAL
CHEF DE CUISINE ARNOLD RUBIO

This easy ceviche from restaurateur Richard Sandoval is packed with vibrant flavors. Use only the freshest fish when selecting a fillet for ceviche.

Combine the mahi–mahi and salt in a small bowl; add the lime juice, cover, and refrigerate for 1 hour.

Combine the orange juice, honey, and ketchup in a small bowl and stir until well mixed. Add the orange juice, onions, tomatoes, and cilantro to the fish and stir together. Season with hot sauce to taste.

To serve, spoon ceviche with a slotted spoon into individual bowls or cups.

Pan-Fried Polenta with Grilled Pears and Gorgonzola Sauce

SALT, BOULDER ❧ EXECUTIVE CHEF BRADFORD HEAP

SALT has made its home on the historic corner of Pearl Street in Boulder where Tom's Tavern sat for forty years, and Chef Bradford Heap has created a menu sourced from local organic farmers whenever possible. In this savory appetizer, crispy polenta complements the classic pairing of Gorgonzola and pears.

2 tablespoons extra virgin olive oil

1 medium onion, finely minced

4 cups water

1 cup uncooked polenta

Salt

½ cup half-and-half

6 ounces Gorgonzola cheese

Extra virgin olive oil,
    for frying polenta

2 medium pears (ripe and soft
    but not blemished; Comice
    or other variety)

¼ cup pine nuts, toasted

Makes 6 servings

Heat 2 tablespoons olive oil in a medium saucepan over medium heat and cook the onions until tender, about 5 minutes.

Add the water to the saucepan and heat over high heat until boiling; whisk in the polenta, stirring constantly, until polenta begins to thicken. Cover, reduce to simmer, and cook, stirring occasionally, until completely thickened and the grains are tender, about 20 minutes. Season with salt to taste.

Grease an 8 x 8 x 2-inch glass baking dish and pour the polenta into it; smooth the top and refrigerate until cool and firm. Polenta can be made in advance and refrigerated for up to 48 hours.

Heat the half-and-half until boiling, then pour it into a blender; add the Gorgonzola cheese and blend until smooth.

Cut the firm polenta into four squares or circles and fry in a nonstick skillet over medium-high heat until golden brown on both sides.

While polenta is frying, peel, halve, and core the pears, then cut into thick slices. Grill in a nonstick grill pan just until grill marks appear.

To serve, lay slices of grilled pear on top of fried polenta. Top with Gorgonzola sauce and sprinkle with pine nuts. Serve while still warm.

Turnip velouté

1 pound baby turnips,
   peeled and cubed

½ cup cream

4 tablespoons butter

Salt

Bacon vinaigrette

4 thick slices wild boar bacon
   or other high-quality bacon,
   cooked crisp, drained,
   and crumbled

¼ cup sherry vinegar

2 lemons, zested and juiced

1 tablespoon honey

¼ cup extra virgin olive oil, divided

1 tablespoon chopped fresh
   marjoram (or 1 teaspoon
   dried oregano)

1 tablespoon chopped fresh parsley

Salt and pepper

Seared Scallops with Turnip Velouté, Celeriac, Apple, and Fennel Salad, and Wild Boar Bacon Vinaigrette

EAST SIDE BISTRO, CRESTED BUTTE ❧ CHEF KALON WALL

The crisp salad of celeriac, apples, and fennel balances out the richness of the scallops and turnip puree in this unusual appetizer.

For the turnip velouté:
Place the turnips in a medium stockpot, cover with water, and bring to a boil. Reduce heat to simmer and cook until the turnips become soft. Drain the water and return the turnips to the pot; add the cream and butter and heat until butter melts.

Transfer the turnip mixture to a blender and puree until smooth; season with salt to taste. Keep warm until ready to serve.

For the bacon vinaigrette:
Combine the bacon with the sherry vinegar, lemon zest, lemon juice, honey, 1 tablespoon of the olive oil, marjoram, and parsley. Season with salt and pepper to taste.

(continued on page 40)

Scallops

12 fresh scallops, U12 size

2 tablespoons butter

Celeriac, apple, and fennel salad

1 bunch frisée (curly endive), chopped

1 bulb celeriac, peeled, and julienned

1 bulb fennel, trimmed and thinly sliced

1 apple, julienned

Makes 4 servings

For the scallops:

Preheat two large sauté pans on high heat. Pat the scallops dry with paper towels. Season the scallops with salt, pepper, and 1 tablespoon olive oil, and toss to coat evenly. When sauté pans are hot, add 1 tablespoon olive oil to each pan and sear the scallops on one side. When scallops are caramelized golden brown, flip them and add 1 tablespoon butter to each pan; allow the butter to brown. Use a spoon to baste each scallop once or twice with butter, then remove from heat and place on paper towels.

To assemble:

Spoon 2 tablespoons of the turnip velouté in the center of each plate. Arrange three scallops on top of the velouté. Combine the frisée with the celeriac, fennel, and apple in a medium bowl and toss with some bacon vinaigrette; place salad on top of the scallops. Just before serving, drizzle the scallops with more of the vinaigrette.

Ribs

2 racks lamb ribs

1 cup plain yogurt

¼ cup Coca-Cola

2 tablespoons Sriracha chile sauce

1 tablespoon red wine vinegar

1 teaspoon dried oregano

2 tablespoons malt powder

1½ teaspoons chopped garlic

1½ teaspoons brown sugar

Fresh herbs for garnish (optional)

Recado

½ cup pistachios, toasted
    and cooled

¼ cup panko bread crumbs

1 teaspoon ground coriander

2 tablespoons packed mint leaves

¼ teaspoon kosher salt

⅛ teaspoon pepper

1 teaspoon extra virgin olive oil

Spicy Malted Lamb Ribs with Pistachio-Mint Recado and Rose Blossom Yogurt

STEUBEN'S AND VESTA DIPPING GRILL, DENVER
EXECUTIVE CHEF MATT SELBY

When Chef Matt Selby first created this recipe during Steuben's opening months for the restaurant's family meal, he discovered just how well malt powder's deep and complex caramel flavor complements game meats. The dish finally made its way to the menu at Vesta, paired with a smooth yogurt sauce. In Mexican cooking a recado is a complement or provision to a dish, like the finishing rub in this recipe.

For the ribs:
Place the ribs in an extra–large ziplock bag. To make the marinade, combine the yogurt, cola, chile sauce, vinegar, oregano, malt powder, garlic, and brown sugar in a medium bowl and whisk to combine. Pour the marinade into the bag with the ribs, seal it, and knead the bag to mix. Marinate in the refrigerator several hours or overnight, if possible.

Preheat the oven to 250 degrees. Remove the ribs from the bag, reserving the marinade. Place the ribs, curve side down, onto a large baking sheet, and generously sprinkle with salt and pepper. Turn the ribs over and season with salt and pepper again. Loosely cover the ribs with aluminum foil, but don't wrap the foil around the edges of the baking sheet or you will steam the ribs.

Roast the ribs for 3 hours, basting with reserved marinade every 15 to 30 minutes. Remove the foil for the last 15 to 30 minutes to caramelize the ribs.

(continued on page 42)

Rose blossom yogurt

½ cup plain yogurt

2 teaspoons ground coriander

¼ teaspoon rose blossom water

1 ½ teaspoons sugar

¼ teaspoon kosher salt

Makes 4 servings

Remove ribs from the oven and, using tongs, press each rack, curve side down, into the pistachio-mint recado. Slice the ribs and garnish with snipped chives, chopped mint, or oregano. Serve with rose blossom yogurt.

For the recado:
Combine all ingredients except the olive oil in a food processor and pulse until coarsely ground and well mixed. With the processor turned on, drizzle in the olive oil.

For the rose blossom yogurt:
Combine all ingredients in a small bowl and whisk until blended.

Falafel

2 pounds peeled, cooked sweet
    potatoes (weight after peeling)

1 tablespoon ground cumin, toasted

3 garlic cloves, chopped

1 tablespoon ground coriander,
    toasted

1 bunch cilantro, chopped

1 lemon, zested and juiced

1 tablespoon olive oil

1 tablespoon salt

Pinch cayenne pepper

1 cup chickpea flour, or more
    as needed

2 (15-ounce) cans chickpeas,
    pureed in a food processor

¼ teaspoon pepper

Grape seed or canola oil, for frying

Lemon-tahini yogurt

8 ounces organic plain yogurt

2½ tablespoons tahini

½ teaspoon salt

1 lemon, zested and juiced

⅛ teaspoon pepper

½ teaspoon sugar

Yields 30 falafel

Sweet Potato Falafel with Lemon-Tahini Yogurt

ROOT DOWN, DENVER   ❧   OWNER AND CHEF JUSTIN CUCCI

Root Down is one of the many great restaurants in Denver that follows a "field to fork" mentality, leaning toward organic, natural, and local ingredients whenever possible. This riff on falafel is gluten-free yet packed with interesting flavors. Leftover falafel may be frozen.

For the falafel:
Combine the sweet potatoes, cumin, garlic, coriander, cilantro, lemon zest, lemon juice, olive oil, salt, cayenne, chickpea flour, chickpeas, and pepper in a large bowl and mix well. Mash until the mixture is smooth with no lumps remaining. Refrigerate for at least 1 hour.

Using a ¼-cup measuring cup, scoop out even portions of the sweet potato batter and form into patties, adding more chickpea flour if the consistency seems too wet. The batter should be moist, but should not stick to your hands.

Heat ½-inch depth of grape seed or canola oil in a large skillet over medium-high heat. When a small portion of batter sizzles in the oil, the oil is sufficiently hot. Fry the falafel patties until golden brown, about 2 minutes per side. Serve with lemon-tahini yogurt.

For the lemon-tahini yogurt:
Combine all ingredients in a small bowl and stir until well mixed.

2 large tomatoes, diced

4 green onions, chopped

1 red bell pepper, minced

3 jalapeños, seeded and minced

1 onion, diced

2 limes, zested and juiced

1 orange, juiced

2 garlic cloves, minced

1 tablespoon garlic powder

2 teaspoons dried oregano

2 tablespoons tequila

Salt and pepper

2 to 3 teaspoons Sriracha
    chile sauce

Yields about 4 cups

Tequila-Lime Salsa

JENNY MORRIS, DENVER

*As soon as my daughter, a food blogger and culinary student, made
this salsa for me, I knew it was a winner. The cool, slightly tangy salsa
is highlighted with just a kiss of tequila and complements many of the
Mexican recipes in this book.*

Combine tomatoes, green onions, red pepper, jalapeños, diced
onion, lime zest, lime juice, orange juice, garlic, garlic powder,
oregano, and tequila in a medium bowl and stir until well mixed.
Season with salt and pepper and Sriracha chile sauce to taste.

Let salsa stand for an hour at room temperature (or up to overnight in the refrigerator) for flavors to meld before serving. Unused
salsa may be stored in a covered container in the refrigerator for
a few days.

❧ **Note:** *If you prefer a smoother salsa, pour combined ingredients into
    a food processor and pulse to desired texture.*

Salads & Sides

Farro and Barley "Risotto," p. 50

Salad

2 pounds fresh baby spinach

1 head Bibb lettuce, torn into
    bite-size pieces

1 pint grape tomatoes,
    halved lengthwise

1½ ounces daikon radish sprouts,
    rinsed and cut

½ cup shredded carrots

½ cup dried cranberries

½ cup pepita seeds, toasted

Dressing

½ cup buttermilk

2 tablespoons half-and-half

¾ cup mayonnaise

6 tablespoons sour cream

1 teaspoon pureed chipotle chiles,
    or more to taste (see Guidelines
    for Recipes on page xviii)

1 teaspoon rice wine vinegar

½ teaspoon lemon juice

½ teaspoon garlic powder

½ teaspoon onion powder

1 teaspoon honey

Dash Tabasco sauce, or more to taste

1 teaspoon chopped fresh parsley

Kosher salt

Pepper

Makes 4 servings;
dressing yields about 2 cups

Baby Spinach and Bibb Lettuce Salad with Chipotle-Buttermilk Dressing

HOTEL BOULDERADO, BOULDER
EXECUTIVE CHEF PETER M. MORRISON

The combination of chipotle seasoning and buttermilk creates a wonderfully flavored salad dressing that just might become your new favorite.

For the salad:
Toss the spinach and Bibb lettuce together and divide equally among four plates. Arrange the grape tomato halves on the salad mix. Place the daikon sprouts in the middle of the salad. Divide the carrots equally among each salad and sprinkle the dried cranberries and toasted pepita seeds on top. Serve with chipotle–buttermilk dressing.

For the dressing:
Combine all ingredients except salt and pepper in the blender and blend until smooth; season to taste with salt and pepper.

1 tablespoon butter

2 cups cauliflower florets

3 cups grilled sweet corn kernels

¼ cup roasted red peppers

Salt and pepper

½ cup grated Parmesan cheese

Makes 6 servings

Cauliflower and Summer Vegetables

PANZANO, HOTEL MONACO, DENVER
EXECUTIVE CHEF ELISE WIGGINS

Chef Elise Wiggins brings the classically simple yet refined flavors of Italy to her restaurant, as you'll find in this easy summer vegetable recipe.

Heat a large skillet over medium-high heat. Add the butter, cauliflower, corn, and peppers and sauté until vegetables are tender-crisp. Season with salt and pepper to taste and finish by tossing with Parmesan cheese.

Salad

2 cups gnocchi

2 tablespoons olive oil

2 tablespoons butter

2 tablespoons minced shallots

2 cups sliced wild mushrooms
(see Note)

2 cups sliced asparagus, blanched

Salt and pepper

4 cups mixed baby lettuces
(preferably organic)

Parmigiano-Reggiano cheese,
for garnish

White truffle oil, for garnish
(optional)

Oregano vinaigrette

2 tablespoons chopped shallots

1 tablespoon Dijon-style mustard

2 tablespoons fresh oregano

2 tablespoons Champagne vinegar
or white wine vinegar

¾ cup extra virgin olive oil

Salt and pepper

Makes 4 servings

Crisp Gnocchi Salad with Wild Mushrooms and Asparagus

SIX89, CARBONDALE   ❧   CHEF MARK FISCHER

Since 1998, Six89 has been serving up really creative food—what they call seasonally based artisanal comfort food—to residents and visitors to Carbondale, located just outside Aspen. While Six89 makes their gnocchi in house, the recipe here calls for premade gnocchi to save time.

For the salad:
Heat a large stockpot of salted water to boiling and blanch the gnocchi for 2 minutes; drain and set aside. Heat the oil and butter over medium-high heat in a heavy-bottomed skillet until nutty brown, taking care not to burn. Add the shallots and gnocchi and cook, stirring often, until the gnocchi begins to color lightly, about 5 minutes. Add the mushrooms and cook until soft, about 5 minutes longer. Add the asparagus and heat through. Season with salt and pepper to taste and toss with 4 to 6 tablespoons of the oregano vinaigrette.

For the oregano vinaigrette:
Mix the shallots, mustard, oregano, and vinegar together in a small bowl. Whisk in the olive oil to emulsify (or shake well in a covered container) and season with salt and pepper to taste.

Presentation:
Place the gnocchi on a serving plate or arrange on individual plates; top with baby lettuces tossed with the oregano vinaigrette. Grate Parmigiano-Reggiano cheese over the top and drizzle with white truffle oil.

❧ *Note: Chanterelles, cepes, morels, and trumpets are all fabulous in this salad, but you may use any mushrooms you like, including crimini, shiitake, or white button mushrooms.*

Extra virgin olive oil

3 to 4 eggplants, peeled, seeded, and diced into ½-inch pieces (about 2½ pounds)

1 cup minced white onion

½ cup minced celery

¼ cup tomato puree

4 tomatoes, seeded and diced into ¼-inch pieces

2 tablespoons tomato paste

2 teaspoons salt

1 to 2 teaspoons chili paste, to taste

Makes 8 servings

Eggplant Caponata

EIGHT K, VICEROY HOTEL, SNOWMASS VILLAGE
EXECUTIVE CHEF ROB ZACK

The restaurant at the Viceroy Hotel gets its name from the elevation of Snowmass, just over 8,000 feet.

Heat a large saucepan over medium–high heat; add enough olive oil just to coat the bottom of the pan. When the oil is hot, carefully add the eggplant and cook, stirring frequently, until soft and browned, about 15 minutes. Remove the eggplant from the pan and set aside.

Add the onion and celery to the same pan and sauté over medium–high heat, adding more olive oil as needed, until vegetables are soft and translucent. Return the eggplant to the pan and add the tomato puree, diced tomatoes, tomato paste, salt, and chili paste; stir to combine. Reduce heat to simmer and cook until the caponata has a thick consistency, about 15 minutes. Serve at room temperature.

1/4 cup uncooked farro

1/4 cup uncooked barley

1 tablespoon extra virgin olive oil

1/4 cup diced leek

1/4 cup diced carrot

1/4 cup diced celery

1/2 cup chicken stock

1/2 cup heavy cream

1/2 cup chopped fresh parsley

1/2 cup grated Parmigiano-Reggiano cheese

Salt and pepper

Makes 4 servings

Farro and Barley "Risotto"

EIGHT K, VICEROY HOTEL, SNOWMASS VILLAGE
EXECUTIVE CHEF ROB ZACK

Chef Rob Zack cleverly uses a combination of whole grains—barley and farro—to create a rich-tasting, hearty, and unusual riff on a classic risotto.

Cook the farro and pearled barley separately with 2 to 3 parts water to grain, until the grains are plump and tender. Drain any liquid that remains and rinse under cold water.

Heat a medium saucepan over medium heat. Add the olive oil, leek, carrot, and celery and sauté until soft. Add the barley and farro, stir together, and cook for 1 minute.

Add the stock and heavy cream and cook until the liquid thickens and the risotto has a nice creamy texture, about 5 to 10 minutes. Stir in the parsley and cheese and season with salt and pepper to taste.

(see photograph on page 45)

2 cups dried black beans
   (sometimes called turtle beans)

3 to 4 quarts water

1 yellow onion, finely chopped

2 garlic cloves, crushed

1 ham hock

2 green bell peppers,
   seeded and chopped

2 bay leaves

¼ teaspoon ground cloves

¼ teaspoon pepper

½ cup extra virgin olive oil
   or canola oil

½ cup white vinegar

Salt

Makes 6 to 8 servings

The Fort's™
Famous Black Beans

THE FORT™, MORRISON
PROPRIETRESS HOLLY ARNOLD KINNEY

When Luis Bonachea was a manager at The Fort™ in the 1960s, he brought his Cuban influence to this dish, which has been on the menu ever since.

Rinse the beans thoroughly, removing any gravel or broken beans. Soak the beans overnight in enough water to cover them by 4 inches.

Drain and rinse the beans, and place them in a stockpot with the 3 to 4 quarts of fresh water (enough to just cover them). Add the onions, garlic, ham hock, bell peppers, bay leaves, cloves, and pepper. Cover and bring just barely to a boil; reduce heat to a very low simmer and cook until beans are tender, about 2 to 4 hours. Check beans frequently, and if the liquid level has dropped so as to threaten to expose the beans, add more hot water. Keep heat low (a rolling boil will break the beans) and stir occasionally to prevent burning.

When the beans have softened, remove the ham hock and separate the meat from the bone. Finely chop the meat and add to the beans. Add the oil and vinegar and simmer 30 minutes longer. Just before serving, remove the bay leaves and season with salt to taste.

Salad

4 heads frisée (curly endive), cleaned and trimmed

8 ounces cured salmon slices, recipe below, or use store-bought

4 poached eggs

Dressing

1 shallot, chopped

2 garlic cloves, chopped

1 teaspoon Dijon-style mustard

1 teaspoon prepared stone-ground mustard

½ cup white balsamic vinegar

1½ to 2 cups extra virgin olive oil, to taste

Cured salmon

½ cup kosher salt

⅔ cup sugar

4 garlic cloves, crushed

1 lemon, sliced

3 pounds salmon, skin on

Makes 4 servings

Frisée Salmon Salad

BITTERSWEET, DENVER   ∾   CHEF OLAV PETERSON

To establish Bittersweet, Chef Olav Peterson took over an abandoned garage in the heart of Denver and converted it to a small restaurant complete with on-site gardens. He cures his own salmon for this salad, but you may use store-bought cured salmon if pressed for time.

For the salad:
Combine the frisée and vinaigrette in a large bowl and toss well. Divide equally among four plates and top each with a poached egg and several slices of cured salmon.

For the dressing:
To make the vinaigrette, combine the shallot, garlic, mustards, and vinegar in a blender and blend until smooth. With blender running, slowly add the desired amount of olive oil until incorporated.

For the cured salmon:
To create the cure, combine the salt, sugar, and garlic in a small bowl and mix well; rub one-fourth of the cure on the skin side of the fish. Place the salmon skin side down in a 13 x 9 x 2-inch glass baking dish and rub the remaining cure on the flesh side of the salmon. Lay lemon slices on top and cover with plastic wrap.

Refrigerate for about a week, turning the fish every 3 days until the flesh feels firm. Rinse off the cure and pat dry. Refrigerate for up to 1 week or freeze until needed.

2 tablespoons canola oil

1 teaspoon minced fresh ginger

1 teaspoon minced garlic

2 cups sugar snap peas

2 cups pea shoots (see Note)

½ teaspoon freshly squeezed
    lime juice

1 tablespoon butter

Salt

Makes 6 servings

Gingered Peas

BLACKBELLY CATERING, BOULDER
FOUNDER/CHEF HOSEA ROSENBERG

*Boulder residents cheered when Chef Hosea Rosenberg took home the title
of* Top Chef *from Bravo TV's* Top Chef, Season Five. *Since the win,
he has launched a catering company and farm, with a restaurant soon
to follow, under the Blackbelly brand.*

Heat a large skillet over high heat and add the oil. Sauté the ginger
and garlic until fragrant, about 1 minute. Add the peas and sauté for
about 2 minutes. Add the pea shoots and toss to just warm through,
about 1 minute, and then stir in the lime juice and butter; season
with salt to taste.

❧ **Note:** *Pea shoots are the early tendril of the pea plant; because they can be
    somewhat hard to find, you may substitute watercress, which is generally
    more available.*

3 ripe peaches, pitted and cut
  into quarters (skin on or off
  as desired)

⅓ cup white balsamic vinegar

1 tablespoon honey

⅔ cup extra virgin olive oil

Salt and freshly cracked pepper

8 cups baby arugula

¼ pound Serrano ham or prosciutto,
  sliced paper thin

Makes 4 servings

Grilled Palisade Peaches, Serrano Ham, and Rocket Salad

LARKSPUR RESTAURANT, VAIL
CULINARY DIRECTOR THOMAS SALAMUNOVICH

In August, when the succulent Palisade peaches come into season in Colorado, restaurants across the state serve them in everything from appetizers to dessert.

Preheat the grill to high heat. Lightly brush the peach quarters with olive oil and quickly grill to achieve grill marks. Let cool to room temperature.

To make the vinaigrette, whisk the vinegar and honey together in a small bowl. Slowly whisk in olive oil until well combined. Season with salt and pepper to taste.

Lightly dress the arugula and peaches separately with the vinaigrette, reserving extra vinaigrette in the refrigerator for another use. Arrange the peaches and arugula in a serving dish or on individual plates. Drape ham around the salad and serve.

Salad

3 small eggplants, sliced into 24 slices

Kosher salt

2 cups flour

5 large eggs, beaten

4 cups panko bread crumbs

Peanut oil, for frying

⅓ cup sherry vinegar

⅔ cup canola oil

1 small shallot, minced

Salt and pepper

4 cups baby arugula

6 heirloom tomatoes, varied colors if available, sliced into 24 thick slices

Fleur de Sel

12 ounces Fruition Farms ricotta or other high-quality whole milk ricotta *(see Sources on page 154)*

Heirloom Tomato Salad with Fruition Farms Ricotta, Eggplant Croutons, Arugula, and Romesco Vinaigrette

FRUITION RESTAURANT, DENVER
OWNER AND CHEF ALEX SEIDEL

Perhaps nobody in Colorado has taken such a public stance on farm-to-table cooking as Chef Alex Seidel, and the result is a passionate staff at his restaurant creating world-class cuisine out of locally grown and sourced ingredients. If you can find it, his creamy sheep's milk ricotta is irresistible.

For the salad:
One to two hours in advance, toss eggplant slices liberally with kosher salt to soften flesh and draw out moisture. Set the slices in a colander to drain.

Remove the slices and pat dry. Bread the eggplant slices by dipping each into flour, then egg, then bread crumbs. Heat peanut oil in a large skillet over medium–high heat and fry the eggplant in batches until golden brown on both sides. Remove to paper towels to soak up excess oil.

Combine the sherry vinegar, canola oil, and shallot and whisk until well mixed; season with salt and pepper to taste. Toss arugula with the desired amount of dressing and mound onto eight salad plates. Top each plate with three fried eggplant slices and three tomato slices; sprinkle with Fleur de Sel to taste. Spoon ricotta onto the plates and serve with Romesco vinaigrette.

Romesco vinaigrette

2 cups roasted red bell peppers

1 cup San Marzano tomatoes
    or other high-quality canned
    tomatoes

2 garlic cloves, minced

2 roasted garlic cloves, minced

1 cup Marcona almonds

¼ cup chopped fresh parsley

Extra virgin olive oil

Sherry vinegar

Salt and pepper

Makes 8 servings

For the Romesco vinaigrette:
Place bell peppers, tomatoes, garlic, and almonds in a food processor and pulse to chop ingredients roughly and blend together. Pour the Romesco into a medium bowl, add the chopped parsley, then the olive oil and sherry vinegar to taste; stir together and season with salt and pepper to taste.

3 tablespoons extra virgin olive oil, divided

1 cup Arborio rice

¼ cup white wine

3 to 4 cups hot chicken stock

½ pound asparagus, trimmed and thinly sliced

1 tablespoon lemon zest

4 small shallots, minced

¼ cup freshly squeezed lemon juice

4 tablespoons butter

¼ cup chopped fresh flat-leaf parsley

Salt and pepper

Makes 4 servings

Lemon and Asparagus Risotto

THE CABIN, THE STEAMBOAT GRAND, STEAMBOAT SPRINGS
CHEF ERIC HYSLOP

Lemon zest and juice perfectly complement the asparagus in this creamy risotto. Use high-quality Arborio rice for the best texture.

Heat 1 tablespoon of the olive oil in a large saucepan over medium-high heat. Add the rice and cook, stirring constantly, until translucent. Deglaze the pan by adding the white wine and gently scraping the bottom of the pan. Slowly add the chicken stock, in small increments, stirring fairly constantly, until rice is nearly cooked and liquid is absorbed. (Do not add more stock until the previous addition is absorbed.) Reserve at least ¼ cup of the stock to finish the dish. The risotto should have a creamy, not sticky, texture.

Heat the remaining 2 tablespoons of oil in a large sauté pan and add the sliced asparagus, lemon zest, minced shallots, and lemon juice. Add the cooked risotto and a bit more hot chicken stock; stir together and cook until rice is tender and liquid is absorbed. Finish by stirring in butter and chopped parsley; season with salt and pepper to taste.

Risotto

2 tablespoons extra virgin olive oil

1 small onion, minced

1 garlic clove, minced

2 cups Carnaroli or Arborio rice

½ cup white wine

7 cups hot veal or chicken stock

1 pound wild mushrooms of choice, sautéed in butter until nicely caramelized

3 tablespoons butter

2 tablespoons chopped fresh parsley

2 tablespoons chopped fresh tarragon

1 cup grated Parmesan cheese

Salt

Sauce

½ cup (1 stick) butter

¼ cup heavy cream

¼ cup chicken stock

Salt and pepper

Makes 8 servings

Mushroom and Brown Butter Risotto

KELLY LIKEN, VAIL   ❧   CHEF/OWNER KELLY LIKEN

The food created by Chef Kelly Liken, nominated for the James Beard Best Chef Southwest award, continues to win over diners at her popular restaurant in the heart of Vail.

For the risotto:
Heat olive oil in a large, heavy-bottomed saucepan over low heat. Cook the onions and garlic until very soft, about 20 minutes, making sure they do not brown.

Increase the heat to medium and add the rice; cook until translucent, about 2 to 3 minutes. Add the wine, stir, and cook until quite dry.

Add the stock in small increments, stirring constantly, until all liquid is absorbed. (Do not add more stock until the previous addition has been completely absorbed.) Continue to add stock and cook, stirring constantly, until the rice is fully cooked and very creamy, about 25 minutes. Stir in the sautéed mushrooms, butter, parsley, tarragon, and Parmesan cheese; season with salt to taste.

Spoon the risotto into bowls and finish the dish by drizzling brown butter sauce over the risotto.

For the sauce:
Melt the butter in a small saucepan, stirring constantly until the butter is a deep nutty brown but not burned. Slowly whisk in the cream to incorporate (taking care as the mixture will foam up), then continue stirring vigorously. Add the chicken stock all at once and bring the mixture to a boil to complete the emulsification of the sauce. Season the sauce with salt and pepper to taste and cover to keep warm for serving.

Olathe Sweet Corn Spoon Bread

LA TOUR, VAIL   ❧   CHEF/PROPRIETOR PAUL FERZACCA

The farms around Olathe produce some of the best sweet corn in the state. At La Tour, it's used in this delicious spoon bread that gets a touch of interesting texture from the addition of wild rice.

¼ cup wild rice

1 quart water

4 tablespoons butter

½ cup diced yellow onion

3 cups whole milk

1 cup sweet corn kernels

2 green onions, chopped

2 teaspoons chopped fresh
    flat-leaf parsley

1½ teaspoons kosher salt

1 teaspoon sugar

¼ teaspoon black pepper

Pinch cayenne pepper

¼ cup cornmeal

2 large eggs

½ cup flour

¼ teaspoon baking powder

Makes 6 to 8 servings

Preheat the oven to 375 degrees. Grease a 3-quart casserole dish.

Combine the wild rice and water in a small saucepan over medium heat and bring to a simmer; cook until the rice has completely popped and is very tender, about 30 to 40 minutes. Drain the rice and spread out on a baking sheet or cutting board to cool.

Melt the butter in a medium saucepan over medium heat; add the onions and cook until translucent. Add the milk and bring to a simmer. Stir in the cooked wild rice, corn, green onion, parsley, salt, sugar, black pepper, and cayenne and bring to simmer; cook about 3 minutes.

While constantly whisking to avoid lumps, slowly sprinkle the cornmeal over top of the milk mixture. Allow the cornmeal to cook for about 5 minutes until thickened, stirring constantly to avoid scorching. Remove from heat and let cool to room temperature.

While the cornmeal mixture is cooling, place the eggs in a small mixing bowl and whip using an electric mixer on high speed until the eggs reach the ribbon stage (when lifted up, the whipped eggs fall back onto themselves like ribbons and are light in color). Sift the flour and baking powder together in a separate bowl, and then gently fold into the cornmeal mixture. Fold in the whipped eggs.

Transfer mixture to the prepared casserole dish and place the dish on a baking sheet to prevent spills in the oven. Bake, uncovered, until top is golden brown and a toothpick inserted in the center comes out clean, about 30 to 45 minutes.

2 pounds white potatoes,
   peeled and quartered

2 tablespoons butter

1 ounce fresh chives

4 ounces roasted poblano peppers,
   skin and seeds discarded

1 cup heavy cream

1 tablespoon salt

Makes 6 to 8 servings

Poblano Chile and Chive Mashed Potatoes

TAMAYO, DENVER
EXECUTIVE CHEF RICHARD SANDOVAL
CHEF DE CUISINE ARNOLD RUBIO

The addition of roasted poblano peppers takes these mashed potatoes from simple to spectacular.

Bring a large pot of water to boil; add the potatoes and cook for 45 minutes. Drain the potatoes in a colander, then place in a large bowl; add butter and mash. Combine the chives, peppers, cream, and salt in a blender and blend until smooth. Pour the mixture into the potatoes and stir to combine.

1 tablespoon extra virgin olive oil

½ cup fresh sage leaves,
    cut into thin strips

½ medium onion, diced

2 Portobello mushrooms,
    gills removed and sliced

1 ½ tablespoons minced garlic

Juice of 1 lemon
    (about 3 tablespoons)

½ teaspoon salt

¼ teaspoon pepper

6 large eggs, beaten

2 cups grated Parmigiano-Reggiano
    cheese

1 pint heavy cream

8 cups torn day-old bread,
    about 1 loaf

Makes 12 servings

Portobello and Sage Bread Pudding

TABLES ON KEARNEY, DENVER
CHEFS AND OWNERS AMY VITALE AND DUSTIN BARRETT

Sage, mushrooms, and Parmigiano-Reggiano cheese come together beautifully in this rich, savory bread pudding. Try serving it instead of a traditional stuffing for your next Thanksgiving dinner.

Preheat the oven to 350 degrees. Butter a 12 x 9 x 2-inch glass baking dish.

Heat the olive oil in a skillet over medium–high heat and add the sage, onion, mushrooms, and garlic; sauté until slightly softened. Add the lemon juice, salt, and pepper and stir to combine. Combine the eggs, cheese, and cream in a large bowl, then stir in the sautéed vegetables. Add the torn bread and stir to mix well.

Pour mixture into the prepared baking dish, cover with aluminum foil, and place the baking dish in a larger pan. Add hot water to the larger pan halfway up the side of the baking dish to create a water bath. Bake for 45 minutes; remove the foil and bake, uncovered, for 15 minutes longer.

1 cup rainbow quinoa,
   (mix of red, black, and white)

1 cup diced bell peppers
   (red, green, yellow, or a mix)

½ small red onion, diced

2 Anaheim chiles, diced

1 (14-ounce) can black beans,
   rinsed and drained

1 cup charred corn kernels

1 teaspoon ground cumin

1 tablespoon chopped
   fresh thyme leaves

½ cup chopped fresh parsley

Zest and juice of 2 limes

Juice of 1 small orange

Juice of 1 small lemon

1 small garlic clove, minced

Salt and pepper

Makes 6 to 8 servings

Quinoa, Black Bean, and Corn Pilaf

9545 RESTAURANT, THE INN AT LOST CREEK,
MOUNTAIN VILLAGE IN TELLURIDE   ❧   CHEF CHAD DILLON

The combination of fresh vegetables and quinoa with citrus and seasonings in this recipe creates a brightly flavored side dish that can also fill in as a vegetarian entrée.

Cook quinoa according to package directions. Combine with remaining ingredients and sauté just until vegetables are tender–crisp. Season with salt and pepper to taste.

1 large boneless chicken breast

Salt

Pepper

Ground cumin

Chili powder

1 cup lightly packed torn
   Romaine lettuce

1 cup lightly packed mixed
   salad greens

1 cup lightly packed torn green
   leaf lettuce

1 cup lightly packed fresh spinach

¼ cup shredded purple cabbage

¼ cup shredded zucchini

¼ cup shredded carrots

¼ cup canned black beans,
   drained and rinsed

¼ cup sliced jicama

2 tablespoons diced tomatoes

¼ cup blue corn tortilla strips
   or chips

¼ cup mango salsa (see Note)

Alpine Avocado Vinaigrette
   (see Sources on page 154)
   or other vinaigrette

Makes 2 servings

Sante Fe Chicken Salad

THE VILLAGE SMITHY, CARBONDALE JARED ETTELSON

The Smithy serves this big bowl salad with Carbondale's own Alpine Avocado Vinaigrette, but you may make your own dressing or substitute another dressing of choice.

Heat grill to medium heat. Season chicken breast with salt, pepper, cumin, and chili powder and grill until cooked and juices run clear. Allow the meat to rest, covered in foil, while you prepare the salad.

Combine all greens in a large bowl, then mix in the cabbage, zucchini, and carrots. Divide evenly between two dinner plates. Top each with black beans, jicama, tomatoes, and tortilla strips.

Slice the grilled chicken breast and divide between the two salads; top with mango salsa and serve with Alpine Avocado Vinaigrette or other vinaigrette of your choice.

❧ **Note:** *To prepare a simple mango salsa, combine 1 diced mango with 1 tablespoon finely minced red onion, 1 minced jalapeño, the juice of 1 lime, and a bit of chopped cilantro.*

2 pounds fresh Brussels sprouts

12 ounces chestnuts, broken into small pieces *(see Note)*

6 tablespoons unsalted butter

¼ cup veal or beef stock

Salt and pepper

Makes 6 servings

Sautéed Brussels Sprouts with Chestnuts

C LAZY U RANCH, GRANBY ❧ CHEF DENNIS KANIGER

Located just outside of Rocky Mountain National Park near Lake Granby, C Lazy U Ranch gives guests an opportunity to experience the traditions of the great American West through dude ranch vacations for families.

Peel off any discolored leaves from the Brussels sprouts and cut off rough stem end. Very thinly slice Brussels sprouts from top to stem using a knife or mandoline.

Heat a large skillet over medium-high heat and melt 4 tablespoons of the butter until browned. Add the Brussels sprouts and chestnuts and cook undisturbed until lightly browned, about 5 minutes. Stir once to allow additional browning for a couple more minutes.

Add the stock and let simmer until liquid is almost completely evaporated. Stir in the remaining butter and season with salt and pepper to taste.

❧ **Note:** *If using dried chestnuts, simmer in lightly salted water about 4 hours to soften; drain before using.*

1 spaghetti squash (about 3 cups
    cooked squash)

Olive oil

1 cup grated Parmesan cheese

4 cups panko bread crumbs

1 tablespoon salt

1 teaspoon white pepper

2 tablespoons basil,
    cut into thin strips

6 large eggs

Canola oil, for frying

Yields about 4 dozen fritters

Spaghetti Squash Fritters

CAFÉ DIVA, STEAMBOAT SPRINGS
EXECUTIVE CHEF KATE RENCH

Chef Kate Rench serves these savory fritters with a farmers' market rata-touille. Try the Eggplant Caponata recipe on page 49 with the fritters or pair the fritters with an herbed sour cream for dipping. Extra fritters may be frozen and reheated in the oven.

Preheat the oven to 450 degrees. Cut the spaghetti squash in half and remove the seeds with a spoon. Rub the cut side with olive oil and place cut side down on a nonstick baking sheet. Roast until squash is cooked (flesh will flake easily with a fork), about 30 to 60 minutes. Remove from oven and cool.

When squash is cool enough to handle, use a fork to pull the strands of squash from the shell. Place strands in a colander and extract all of the water out of the squash by pressing very hard.

Combine the squash with the Parmesan, bread crumbs, salt, white pepper, basil, and eggs in a large bowl and stir together to make the dough.

Heat about 4 inches of canola oil in a deep stockpot over medium–high heat. Shape the dough into silver dollar–size balls.

When oil is hot enough that a small piece of dough sizzles, fry the fritters in batches until golden brown. Remove each batch to a paper towel to drain. Fritters may be made ahead and reheated in the oven for a party.

4¼ cups half-and-half

2 tablespoons butter

1 cup stone-ground organic
   white corn grits
   (see Sources on page 154)

4 ounces blue vein goat cheese
   (see Sources on page 154)

½ tablespoon kosher salt

½ tablespoon pepper

Makes 4 to 6 servings

Stone-Ground Bleu Cheese Grits

8100 MOUNTAINSIDE BAR & GRILL,
PARK HYATT BEAVER CREEK RESORT AND SPA, BEAVER CREEK
EXECUTIVE CHEF CHRISTIAN APETZ

Chef Christian Apetz is as passionate about the ingredients he uses as he is about the food he prepares. He prefers Anson Mills grits over other brands and believes these bleu cheese grits are so fabulous they'll never come off the menu at his restaurant. One taste and you'll probably agree.

Combine half-and-half and butter in a large, heavy-gauge saucepan over medium-high heat and bring to a simmer. Whisk in grits and cook on low heat, stirring constantly, until grits thicken and are cooked through, about 4 to 6 minutes. Stir in crumbled blue vein goat cheese and season with the salt and pepper. Serve with your favorite steaks hot off the grill.

⋙ **Note:** *You may substitute any grits and any bleu cheese for this recipe. Be sure to cook grits according to package directions, as cooking time varies greatly from brand to brand.*

Summer Caprese Salad, p. 70

½ cup balsamic vinegar

4 medium heirloom tomatoes, thinly sliced

¼ cup basil pesto

Extra virgin olive oil

8 ounces feta cheese, crumbled

Makes 4 servings

Summer Caprese Salad

PANZANO, HOTEL MONACO, DENVER
EXECUTIVE CHEF ELISE WIGGINS

A simple Caprese salad is a welcome side dish when tomatoes are at their peak during the warm summer days in Colorado. The chef at Panzano makes hers special by adding feta cheese.

Heat vinegar in a small saucepan over medium heat and simmer until it is reduced in half; let cool.

Lay thinly sliced tomatoes around salad plates, slightly overlapping the slices. Stir just enough olive oil into the pesto until it is of salad dressing consistency, and then pour the pesto over the tomatoes. Sprinkle the feta cheese on top and finish by drizzling the balsamic reduction over all.

(see photograph on page 69)

Salad

2 cups diced heirloom tomatoes

1 cup diced or balled watermelon

½ teaspoon chopped fresh
    flat-leaf parsley

½ teaspoon chopped fresh chives

½ teaspoon chopped fresh
    tarragon

2 tablespoons extra virgin olive oil

Salt and pepper

1 teaspoon Fleur de Sel or other
    high-quality sea salt, for garnish

1 tablespoon balsamic vinegar,
    for garnish

6 large fresh basil leaves, cut into
    thin strips, for garnish

Granita

1 fennel bulb, cored and
    thinly sliced

½ cup white wine

Juice of 1 lemon
    (about 3 tablespoons)

½ cup sugar

1 cup water

Makes 4 servings

Tomato and Watermelon Salad with Fennel Granita

OPUS, LITTLETON   ❧   CHEF SEAN MCGAUGHEY

*Longtime residents of the Littleton area were thrilled when Opus opened
as a fine dining restaurant on downtown Littleton's historic Main Street.
This summery salad gets a special boost from the fennel granita, which
can be prepared the day before.*

For the salad:

Toss together the tomatoes, watermelon, parsley, chives, tarragon,
and olive oil in a medium bowl until well combined; season with
salt and pepper to taste. Let the mixture sit at room temperature
for a few minutes for flavors to meld.

Divide the tomato and watermelon salad evenly among four plates,
reserving any juices that remain in the bowl; drizzle juices over each
salad. Garnish each salad with Fleur de Sel, balsamic vinegar, and
basil. Just before serving, top with 2 tablespoons of the fennel granita.

For the granita:

Blanch the fennel in boiling water until tender, about 5 minutes;
drain. Combine the blanched fennel, white wine, lemon juice, sugar,
and water in a small saucepan over medium–high heat and bring
to a boil. Remove from heat and carefully puree hot mixture in a
blender. Strain through a fine-mesh strainer into a small bowl and
discard solids.

Pour the liquid into a wide, flat container and freeze until solid,
scraping with a fork every hour or two to create ice shavings.
To serve, scrape the frozen surface with a spoon and collect
the ice shavings.

6 large vine-ripe tomatoes, peeled

½ medium red onion, finely diced

2 tablespoons chopped
    roasted garlic

1 tablespoon chopped fresh basil

½ cup extra virgin olive oil

2 tablespoons sherry vinegar
    (or red wine vinegar or
    balsamic vinegar)

1 tablespoon brown sugar

Salt and pepper

Makes 6 to 8 servings

Tuscan Marinated Tomatoes

SKI TIP LODGE, KEYSTONE & EXECUTIVE CHEF KEVIN MCCOMBS

Ski Tip Lodge, a former 1800s stagecoach stop transformed into a cozy bed and breakfast, serves a rotating four-course menu to guests who dine here. Serve these marinated tomatoes from one of their summer menus with fish, steak, pasta, salad, or couscous, or as an appetizer over toast points or crostini.

Cut tomatoes into thick slices and remove and discard the seeds. Roughly chop the tomato slices and mix with the onion, garlic, basil, olive oil, vinegar, brown sugar, and salt and pepper to taste. Allow to marinate at room temperature for at least 1 hour or up to 3 days in the refrigerator.

1 pound beets (yellow, red, or a mix)

1 teaspoon cherry or raspberry vinegar

2 teaspoons balsamic vinegar

½ cup extra virgin olive oil

½ cup pistachio or walnut oil

Salt and pepper

1 (6-ounce) log of fresh Haystack Mountain goat cheese (*see Sources on page 154*) or other high-quality goat cheese

1 cup toasted pistachios, chopped small

1 pound arugula

Makes 6 servings

Warm Goat Cheese Salad with Pistachios and Baby Beets

THE PENROSE ROOM AT THE BROADMOOR, COLORADO SPRINGS
EXECUTIVE CHEF BERTRAND BOUQUIN

Roasted beets and goat cheese are a classic combination, and the chefs at The Broadmoor use locally produced Haystack Mountain goat cheese in their salad.

Preheat the oven to 350 degrees. Wash the beets well and wrap in aluminum foil. Bake until tender, about 1 hour, using the tip of a knife to check tenderness. Let cool and then peel the beets; slice into wedges and set aside.

Combine the vinegars in a small bowl and whisk in the olive oil and pistachio oil; season with salt and pepper to taste.

Cut the goat cheese log into six equal slices (thread or dental floss works well for this purpose) and sprinkle the pistachios on the slices. Press pistachios onto the cheese so that they stick to it on all sides. Warm the goat cheese slices in the preheated oven for about 5 minutes.

While the goat cheese is in the oven, toss the beets in some of the dressing in a medium bowl. Toss the arugula in the remaining dressing in a large bowl. Divide the arugula among six plates and top with roasted beets and warm goat cheese.

Salad

1 head iceberg lettuce, outer leaves removed, rinsed and quartered

½ cup bleu cheese crumbles

4 slices thick-cut bacon, fried crisp, drained, and crumbled

4 green onions, thinly sliced

12 to 18 grape tomatoes, halved

Freshly cracked black pepper

Dressing

½ cup mayonnaise

¼ cup buttermilk

¼ cup New Belgium Saison-style beer or other farmhouse ale

1 tablespoon freshly squeezed lemon juice

¾ teaspoon garlic salt

1 teaspoon honey

Makes 4 servings

Wedge Salad with Saison-Ranch Dressing

NEW BELGIUM BREWERY, FORT COLLINS ❧ JESSICA TALLMAN

Employees at New Belgium, the makers of the popular Fat Tire beer, are always thinking up new ways to use their beers in recipes. A Saison-style beer is used in place of vinegar and creates a nice contrast to the creaminess of the mayonnaise in this dressing for a classic wedge salad.

For the salad:
Place the quartered iceberg lettuce in the center of four salad plates and drizzle with Saison–ranch dressing. Dividing evenly between the plates, sprinkle the bleu cheese crumbles, bacon, and green onions over the top of the wedges. Arrange the tomatoes around the base of the salads and the edges of the plates. Sprinkle freshly cracked black pepper on top to taste.

For the dressing:
Combine the mayonnaise, buttermilk, beer, lemon juice, garlic salt, and honey in a small bowl and mix well. Chill until ready to serve.

Soups & Stews

Curried Butternut Squash Soup, p. 81

4 tablespoons butter

1 yellow onion, roughly chopped

6 (16-ounce) cans artichokes
    in water, undrained

1 quart heavy cream

4 ounces Gruyère cheese, shredded

Salt and pepper

8 ounces lump or claw crab meat
    (optional)

Makes 6 to 8 servings

Artichoke Bisque

THE CLIFF HOUSE, MANITOU SPRINGS
EXECUTIVE CHEF SCOTT SAVAGE

Built in 1873, as the town of Manitou Springs expanded during the gold mining days, The Cliff House at Pikes Peak has been open to guests longer than Colorado has been a state. While the restaurant serves this rich soup topped with crab, it's equally delicious on its own.

Heat the butter in a large stockpot over medium-high heat and sauté the onions until soft. Add the artichokes, including the liquid, and the heavy cream and stir together; simmer 1 hour.

Remove from heat and puree the artichoke mixture until smooth using a stick blender or, in batches, in a traditional blender. Add the cheese and blend again.

Because artichokes can be stringy, it is recommended that you pass the soup through a fine-mesh strainer into a large bowl and discard the solids before serving. If you choose not to strain the soup, puree it very well in small batches in a blender.

Season with salt and pepper to taste. Serve the soup with warm crab meat on top.

1 tablespoon extra virgin olive oil

1 tablespoon butter

½ medium red onion, diced

½ medium Spanish onion, diced

1 tablespoon chopped garlic

2½ pounds ground bison

1 tablespoon chili powder, toasted

1 tablespoon ground cumin, toasted

1 poblano pepper, diced small

2 tablespoons tomato paste

1 tablespoon flour

1 tablespoon barbecue sauce

1 tablespoon ketchup

2 cups tomato puree

2 teaspoons sugar (optional)

½ cup cooked pinto beans,
    or more to taste

1 tablespoon chipotle puree
    (see Guidelines for Recipes
    on page xviii)

1 small bay leaf

1 cup chicken or beef stock

Salt and pepper

Shredded cheddar cheese,
    for garnish

Makes 8 servings

Bison Chili

THE RITZ-CARLTON, BACHELOR GULCH, AVON

This popular chili is a staple on the bar menu at the Ritz-Carlton near the Beaver Creek ski resort. You may substitute lean ground beef for the bison.

Heat the olive oil and butter in a large stockpot over medium heat and cook the onions and garlic until softened, about 5 minutes. Add the ground bison and cook until completely browned.

Add the chili powder, cumin, and poblano pepper and stir to combine. Add the tomato paste and stir until well mixed. Stir in the flour, then add the barbecue sauce, ketchup, tomato puree, sugar, beans, chipotle puree, bay leaf, and stock. Simmer over low heat until the meat is completely broken down, about 2 hours.

Remove the bay leaf and season with salt and pepper to taste. Serve with cheddar cheese or other toppings of your choice.

The Ritz-Carlton resort in Beaver Creek owns Anderson's Cabin, situated just above the resort, where private events are hosted. The cabin was the original homestead of John Anderson, one of seven bachelors who settled the gulch in the early 1900s. This group of unmarried men who called what is now "Bachelor Gulch" home made a living logging, grazing cattle, trapping, and hay farming, until the Great Depression.

2 pounds buffalo meat,
    cut into cubes

Salt and pepper

Flour, for dredging

2 tablespoons canola oil

2 medium onions, diced small

1 medium garlic clove, minced

1 tablespoon tomato paste

2 cups straight Kentucky bourbon

½ cup strong black coffee

1 teaspoon minced fresh rosemary

2 teaspoons minced fresh thyme

Salt and pepper

6 small potatoes,
    peeled and quartered

Makes 6 servings

Henry H. "Shorty Scout" Zietz, the founder of the Buckhorn Exchange restaurant, was friends with Col. William F. "Buffalo Bill" Cody and Chief Sitting Bull. The historic eating and drinking establishment catered to "cattlemen, miners, railroad builders, silver barons, Indian chiefs, roustabouts, gamblers, and businessmen" alike.

Buffalo Redeye Stew

THE BUCKHORN EXCHANGE, DENVER   CHEF CESAR GARCIA

The Buckhorn Exchange, now operating in its second century, survived Prohibition, which began in 1916 in Colorado, and after the repeal of the 18th Amendment, was granted Colorado Liquor License No.1, which you can see on display in the restaurant today. It's no surprise, therefore, that this stew includes a strong dose of bourbon. To reduce the intensity of bourbon flavor, replace half or all of the bourbon with beef stock or red wine.

Season the meat with salt and pepper and dredge in flour. Heat the oil in a large, heavy–bottomed pan and brown the meat on all sides.

Add the onions and garlic and cook until the onions are soft. Stir in the tomato paste and cook 1 minute. Add the bourbon and coffee, stir to combine, and add the rosemary, thyme, salt, pepper, and potatoes. Bring to a boil; reduce heat to low, cover, and simmer, stirring occasionally, until the meat is tender, about 1 hour.

  Note: *For a pretty presentation, cut the tops off small pumpkins, hollow out the insides, and fill with stew. Replace the tops for serving.*

2 tablespoons extra virgin olive oil

1 cup diced onion

1 cup diced leeks, white part only

½ cup diced celery

Pinch salt

1 cup peeled and diced potatoes

1 cup roasted garlic cloves
   *(see Guidelines for Recipes
   on page xviii)*

5 (14-ounce) cans chicken stock

Salt and pepper

½ bunch cilantro, chopped,
   or more to taste

1 cup heavy cream, or less to taste

Garlic croutons, for garnish

Makes 8 to 10 servings

Cream of Cilantro Soup

I first had a soup similar to this one while vacationing in Mexico and knew I had to create my own version at home. Using roasted garlic instead of fresh eliminates the heat from raw garlic, and the soup is a perfect starter to a Mexican-themed menu.

Heat the olive oil in a large saucepan over medium heat. Add the onion, leeks, celery, and a pinch salt to draw the water out of the onion. Cover and cook until the vegetables are soft but not brown, about 5 to 10 minutes.

Add the potatoes, garlic, and stock, and season with salt and pepper to taste. Bring to a boil over high heat; reduce to a simmer, cover, and cook until the vegetables are very tender, about 15 minutes.

Remove the pot from the heat, add the cilantro, and puree using a stick blender or, in batches, in a traditional blender. Stir in the cream and cook on medium heat just long enough to heat through. Serve the soup with garlic croutons.

1 large butternut squash
(about 3 pounds)

Canola oil

2 tablespoons extra virgin olive oil,
plus more for garnish

1 large yellow onion, diced

1 large carrot, diced

1 tablespoon Madras-style
curry powder

½ cup heavy cream

2 tablespoons unsalted
organic butter

Kosher salt

Chopped fresh parsley, for garnish

Makes 6 to 8 servings

Curried Butternut Squash Soup

COLTERRA, NIWOT   ❧   EXECUTIVE CHEF BRADFORD HEAP

This tried-and-true soup from Colterra is made with local organic butternut squash. If you prefer, you may omit the curry powder.

Preheat the oven to 375 degrees. Cut the squash in half lengthwise and remove the seeds with a large spoon. Coat the squash evenly with canola oil and place flesh side down on a baking sheet lined with parchment paper. Roast squash in the oven until it is fork tender, about 30 minutes. Remove and let cool.

While the squash is cooling, heat the olive oil in a 4-quart, heavy-bottomed saucepan over medium heat. Add onion and carrot and cook until the onion is translucent, about 5 to 10 minutes. Add the curry powder and cook 1 minute.

Scoop the flesh from the squash and add it to the saucepan. Add just enough cold water to cover the vegetable mixture and bring to a boil, stirring frequently. Reduce heat and simmer for 20 minutes.

Puree the soup until smooth using a stick blender or, in small batches, in a traditional blender. Return the soup to the saucepan and bring to a simmer over low heat, stirring in a little water if the soup is too thick. Whisk in the cream and butter and season with kosher salt to taste. Serve piping hot, garnished with fresh parsley and a drizzle of extra virgin olive oil.

(see photograph on page 75)

3 tablespoons vegetable oil

1 medium onion, roughly chopped

1-inch piece of fresh ginger, minced

4 garlic cloves, chopped

1 teaspoon cumin

2 teaspoons ground coriander

¼ teaspoon ground turmeric

2 medium potatoes,
    peeled and diced

2 heaping cups cauliflower florets

5 cups chicken stock

⅔ cup heavy cream

Salt

Cayenne pepper

Makes 6 servings

Gingery Cauliflower Soup

DUNTON HOT SPRINGS, DOLORES

Dunton Hot Springs is an exclusive resort that was created by meticulously restoring an old mining town turned ghost town. Today, the open kitchen that produces a new menu every day is the heart of what was once the town's famous saloon.

Heat the oil in a large saucepan over medium–high heat and add the onion, ginger, and garlic; cook until the onion is soft.

Add the cumin, coriander, turmeric, potatoes, cauliflower, and chicken stock and stir together. Bring to a boil; reduce to simmer, cover, and cook until the potatoes and cauliflower are tender, about 20 to 30 minutes.

Puree the soup using a stick blender or, in batches, in a traditional blender. Add the cream and stir to combine; season with salt and cayenne to taste.

❧ **Note:** *At Dunton Hot Springs, they strain the pureed soup before adding the cream for a velvety smooth texture, but you may omit this step if desired.*

Pork

1 (4- to 5-pound) pork shoulder roast (boneless or bone in)

5 tablespoons mesquite Liquid Smoke

1 teaspoon salt

2 teaspoons cumin

1 teaspoon ground coriander

2 teaspoons chili powder

Posole

1 (14-ounce) can low-fat beef stock

½ cup extra virgin olive oil

2 (28-ounce) cans cooked hominy, drained and rinsed

1 bunch cilantro, large stems removed, finely chopped

4 ounces tomatillos, pureed

2 (14-ounce) cans stewed Mexican tomatoes

3 bunches scallions, finely chopped

1 tablespoon cumin

Salt and pepper

2 (14-ounce) cans green enchilada sauce

½ to 1 pound roasted chile peppers, skinned and seeded (mild, medium, or hot)

Shredded Mexican cheese, for garnish

Makes 8 to 12 servings

Green Chile Posole

Chili cook-offs are popular in Colorado, and longtime Denver resident Doug Wulf created the original recipe for this posole for a neighborhood chili competition that I was asked to judge; he won first place. Since then, Doug's friends and family have re-created it and won in two other competitions. I've adapted the original recipe to use fresh ingredients where possible.

For the pork roast:
Preheat the oven to 325 degrees. Use a knife to spear the pork roast all over, and then place it on a large piece of heavy-duty aluminum foil. Mix together the Liquid Smoke, salt, cumin, coriander, and chili powder and pour over the roast. Seal the foil tightly and wrap in two more layers of foil.

Place the roast in a broiler pan with an inch of water in the bottom; place entire pan in the oven and cook for 3 hours.

Remove from the oven and let the meat cool slightly while still wrapped in the foil. Shred or cut the pork into bite-size pieces, discarding any chunks of fat or gristle.

For the posole:
Place the pork in a large stockpot and add the stock, olive oil, hominy, cilantro, tomatillo puree, tomatoes, scallions, cumin, salt and pepper to taste, enchilada sauce, and chiles. Stir together, cover, and simmer for 1 hour to bring all the flavors together.

Garnish with cheese or other toppings of your choice. Leftovers freeze well.

1 red onion, diced medium

2 garlic cloves, minced

½ cup extra virgin olive oil, divided

12 tomatillos

1 jalapeño

1 poblano pepper

6 green tomatoes, cored and diced (about 6 cups)

4 cucumbers, peeled, seeded, and roughly chopped (about 4 cups)

Juice of 2 lemons (about 6 tablespoons)

Juice of 2 limes (about 6 tablespoons)

¼ cup sherry vinegar

3 ounces of a baguette, torn into small pieces

1 cup scallions

1 cup mint leaves

1 cup fresh parsley leaves

1 cup fresh cilantro leaves

1 quart water

Salt

Garnishes

Crème fraîche

Toasted pumpkin seeds

Diced avocado

Fresh crab in season

Extra virgin olive oil

Makes 8 servings

Green Gazpacho

AJAX TAVERN, THE LITTLE NELL, ASPEN ❧ CHEF ALLISON JENKINS

Ajax Tavern, with its mountainside patio, is a popular spot for lunch or dinner year-round. This interesting gazpacho, made from all green vegetables, is fabulous served with some crab or other condiments on top.

Cook the onion and garlic in ¼ cup of the olive oil in a small skillet over medium heat; cool to room temperature.

Remove the outer husk from the tomatillos. Blacken tomatillos, the jalapeño, and the poblano pepper on the grill or in a hot cast-iron skillet. Let cool and remove the seeds and skin from the peppers.

Combine the onion and garlic, tomatillos, peppers, tomatoes, cucumbers, lemon juice, lime juice, vinegar, baguette pieces, scallions, mint, parsley, cilantro, and water in a large bowl; toss to mix well and marinate for 15 minutes.

Puree the mixture with a stick blender, traditional blender, food processor, or food mill to desired texture. Add the remaining ¼ cup olive oil and season with salt to taste. Serve chilled either plain or with any combination of garnishes.

3 cups lentils, rinsed

6 cups chicken stock or water

2 tablespoons extra virgin olive oil

1 small onion, finely chopped

Pinch kosher salt

3 celery stalks, finely chopped

2 carrots, finely chopped

2 garlic cloves, minced

1 tablespoon cumin

1 teaspoon ground coriander

1 teaspoon dark chili powder

2 tablespoons extra virgin olive oil

6 thin slices of prosciutto

Makes 8 servings

Lentil Soup with Prosciutto Chips

221 SOUTH OAK, TELLURIDE
CHEF AND OWNER ELIZA H. S. GAVIN

This warming soup with a big kick from cumin is more than able to stand alone, but the prosciutto chips add both salty flavor and crunchy texture.

Combine the lentils and 6 cups of chicken stock or water in a large stockpot over medium-high heat and bring to a boil. Reduce heat to medium and simmer until the lentils are tender, about 2 hours. If the lentils appear to be drying out, add more water as needed. Cooking time will depend on the type of lentils used as well as their age.

When the lentils are nearly cooked, heat the olive oil in a large skillet over medium-high heat; add the onion and a pinch salt and cook until the onion is translucent, about 10 minutes.

Reduce the heat to medium, add the celery and carrots, and continue cooking until the vegetables are soft. Stir in the garlic, cumin, coriander, and chili powder and cook for an additional 3 minutes.

Place the cooked vegetables, 1 cup of the lentils, and 1 cup of the liquid from the soup in a blender and puree until smooth. Pour the puree back into the stockpot with the remaining lentils and heat until the soup bubbles.

While the soup is heating, preheat the oven to 400 degrees. Spread the olive oil on a baking sheet and place the prosciutto slices on the oiled sheet. Bake, watching carefully so that the prosciutto doesn't burn, until the slices are crisp, about 10 minutes. Transfer the crisp prosciutto to paper towels to remove any excess grease and crumble into large pieces. Spoon the soup into bowls and top with prosciutto chips.

Meat

1 whole smoked pheasant or chicken (about 1 pound cooked meat)

3 celery stalks, roughly chopped

2 carrots, peeled and roughly chopped

1 white onion, roughly chopped

1 bay leaf

1 gallon of water

Soup

½ cup (1 stick) butter

2 celery stalks, finely chopped

1 carrot, peeled and finely chopped

1 white onion, finely chopped

1 cup cooked wild rice

1 cup roasted sweet corn kernels

½ cup flour

½ cup dry sherry

3 cups heavy cream

Salt and pepper

Chopped fresh chives, for garnish

Makes 4 servings

Smoked Pheasant Soup

THE STANLEY HOTEL, ESTES PARK
EXECUTIVE CHEF RICHARD BEICHNER
FOOD AND BEVERAGE MANAGER MARK ORTELL

This rich and creamy soup from the Stanley Hotel brims with a pleasant lightly smoky flavor. If you prefer a lighter soup, simply eliminate or reduce the amount of cream at the end. Smoked chicken is often easier to find than pheasant and works just as well in the recipe.

For the meat:
Place the pheasant or chicken, celery, carrots, onion, and bay leaf in a large stockpot and cover with 1 gallon of water; simmer over low heat for 3 hours. Remove from heat and let cool.

When cool, strain the stock through a fine-mesh strainer into a large bowl, reserving 8 cups of the stock. Pull the meat from the carcass and shred or chop finely. Discard skin and bones.

For the soup:
Melt the butter in a large stockpot over medium-high heat. Add the celery, carrots, and onion and cook until all are soft, about 5 minutes.

Add the rice, corn, and flour; stir together and cook until the flour is absorbed into the rest of the ingredients. Stir in the sherry and cook a couple of minutes to evaporate the alcohol.

Add the reserved stock and shredded pheasant or chicken and heat until the mixture boils. Slowly add the heavy cream, stir, return to a simmer, and cook for 5 minutes to thicken slightly. Season with salt and pepper to taste and garnish with chopped chives before serving.

Soup

6 cups organic chicken stock, recipe below, or use store-bought stock

4 eggs, beaten

10 ounces fresh spinach leaves

¾ cup grated Parmigiano-Reggiano cheese

Stock

1 (2½-pound) organic chicken

1 carrot, roughly chopped

1 white onion, roughly chopped

2 celery stalks, roughly chopped

1 gallon water

2 ounces sea salt

Makes 4 servings

Stracciatella

RUSTICO, TELLURIDE   ❧   EXECUTIVE CHEF PAOLO CANCLINI

At Rustico, Chef Paolo Canclini brings a touch of Old World Italy to the resort town of Telluride, which the owners say reminds them of their hometown in the northern Italian Alps. He uses a rich, homemade, organic chicken stock as the base for his popular stracciatella soup. If you're pinched for time, make the stock the day before, or use store-bought stock.

For the soup:
In a stockpot over medium–high heat, bring the stock to a boil; reduce heat to simmer. Stir in the eggs to form ribbons of cooked egg, then stir in the spinach and the Parmigiano-Reggiano cheese; simmer for 5 minutes. Ladle the soup into bowls and serve.

For the stock:
Place chicken, carrot, onion, and celery in a large stockpot and cover with the water; add the salt. Bring water to a boil, reduce heat, and simmer, uncovered, for 3 hours.

Strain the stock through a fine–mesh strainer into a large bowl and reserve to make soup. Once the carcass has cooled, the cooked chicken can be deboned and used in a salad or for cold chicken salad.

Soup

12 ears of sweet corn

1 medium onion, cut into quarters

4 whole garlic cloves

2 sprigs of fresh thyme

1½ gallons water

½ cup (1 stick) butter

1 large onion, diced

Salt and pepper

Juice of 2 lemons
(about 6 tablespoons)

Cilantro puree

2 bunches fresh cilantro, rinsed

4 to 6 tablespoons extra virgin
olive oil

Salt and pepper

Makes 8 servings

Sweet Corn Soup
with Cilantro Puree

MONTAGNA, THE LITTLE NELL, ASPEN
EXECUTIVE CHEF ROBERT G. MCCORMICK

The cilantro puree is a brilliant accent for this velvety smooth corn soup, which gets extra flavor from a stock based on charred corn cobs. You may strain out the solids before serving for an extra-smooth texture, as they do at The Little Nell, but it's not necessary in order to enjoy the flavors of the soup.

For the soup:
Cut the kernels of corn from the cobs and set aside. Grill the cleaned cobs until there is an even charring all over them.

Place the grilled cobs in a large stockpot along with the quartered onion, garlic, and thyme. Add the water, bring to a simmer, and cook for 90 minutes. Strain the corn stock though a fine-mesh strainer into a large bowl and discard solids.

Heat the butter in a large stockpot over medium heat and sweat the diced onion until soft and translucent. Add the corn and cook, stirring occasionally, for 15 minutes.

Add 1 gallon of the reserved corn stock and bring the mixture to a light boil. Reduce heat and simmer until the corn is thoroughly cooked through, about 30 minutes.

Puree the soup using a stick blender or, in batches, in a traditional blender. Season with salt and pepper to taste; stir in the lemon juice. Spoon into bowls and garnish with cilantro puree.

For the cilantro puree:
Bring 1 gallon of salted water to a rapid boil. Add the cilantro and blanch until soft and tender, about 1 minute. Cool in an ice bath and drain.

Roughly chop the cilantro, place in a blender, and puree, adding enough olive oil to form a thick paste; season with salt and pepper to taste.

¼ cup grape seed oil

1 small onion, diced

2 large cloves garlic, sliced

¼ pound thinly sliced shallots
    (about 5 medium shallots)

1 tablespoon minced galangal
    or fresh ginger

1 tablespoon yellow curry powder

½ teaspoon white pepper

1 teaspoon salt

2 (28-ounce) cans peeled tomatoes

8 cups water

⅓ cup palm sugar or brown sugar

2 to 3 stalks fresh lemongrass,
    cut into pieces and bruised

½ cup cilantro stems

¼ ounce kaffir lime leaves, bruised
    (about 5 large leaves)

Makes 8 servings

Tomato-Curry Soup

CHOLON, DENVER LON SYMENSMA

Don't be fooled by the simple title; this soup is nothing like your everyday tomato soup. With hints of ginger, lemongrass, and a very slight curry flavor, it's both refreshing and satisfying and is typical of the Asian-fusion cuisine served at ChoLon.

Heat the oil in a large stockpot over medium–high heat. Add the onion, garlic, shallots, and galangal; reduce heat and sweat the vegetables until very aromatic, but not browned, about 5 minutes.

Add the curry powder, white pepper, and salt and cook until aromatic, about 1 minute. Add the tomatoes, water, and sugar and bring to a simmer.

Wrap the lemongrass, cilantro, and lime leaves in cheesecloth and tie closed to make a bouquet garni; add to the pot. Simmer the soup for 20 minutes, and then remove the bouquet garni and discard.

Puree the soup using a stick blender or, in batches, in a traditional blender. If desired, pass the soup through a fine–mesh strainer before serving for a velvety smooth texture.

Main Courses

Portabello Mushroom Burger, p. 115

2 (5-ounce) fillets of Alamosa striped bass or other mild whitefish

Salt and pepper

2 tablespoons canola oil

1 tablespoon extra virgin olive oil

8 mussels

2 ounces chorizo (about 1 small link)

6 pearl onions

4 large shiitake mushrooms, stems removed and sliced

1 small fennel bulb, thinly sliced

4 asparagus spears, sliced into 2-inch pieces

6 large cherry tomatoes

1 cup carrot juice

½ cup heavy cream

1 tablespoon butter

Popcorn shoots or pea tendrils, for garnish (optional)

Makes 2 servings

Alamosa Striped Bass

ST. REGIS HOTEL, ASPEN   ❧   EXECUTIVE CHEF JASON ADAMS

Alamosa striped bass—farmed by the Faucett family in Alamosa, Colorado—is perhaps the freshest fish available in Colorado and has an excellent mild flavor, making it a popular item on restaurant menus. Any other mild whitefish would be a good substitute.

Preheat the oven to 350 degrees. Score the skin of the bass fillets and season with salt and pepper. Heat the canola oil in a heavy-bottomed, oven-safe skillet over high heat; sear the fillets, skin side down, until crispy. Transfer the skillet to the oven and bake for 5 to 10 minutes to finish cooking.

While the bass is baking, heat the olive oil in a large sauté pan over medium-high heat. Add the mussels, chorizo, onions, mushrooms, and fennel and sauté, stirring occasionally. When the mussels start to open, add the asparagus and cherry tomatoes and cook for 1 minute. Stir in the carrot juice and simmer for 1 minute.

Remove the mussels and vegetables with a slotted spoon and transfer to a warm plate. Stir the cream into the carrot juice and reduce until slightly thickened. Remove the pan from the heat and stir in the butter until melted. Return the mussels and vegetables to the sauce and heat through.

Presentation:
Pour the mixture into a large bowl, place the cooked bass on top, and finish with popcorn shoots.

2 tablespoons extra virgin olive oil

1 (4-pound) pork shoulder

Salt and pepper

4 apples, any type, sliced

1 large white onion, diced

4 celery stalks, diced

1 bottle white wine

1 quart apple juice

1 quart chicken or duck stock

1 tablespoon coriander seeds

1 tablespoon mustard seeds

1 tablespoon black peppercorns

1 cup Dijon-style mustard

1 tablespoon butter

1 apple, julienned, for garnish

1 tablespoon prepared whole-
grain mustard, for garnish

Makes 8 servings

Braised Pork with Apples and Dijon

BAROLO GRILL, DENVER

OWNER BLAIR TAYLOR   ❧   EXECUTIVE CHEF DARREL TRUETT

The classic flavors of pork and apple come together in this dish, accented by hints of mustard in the sauce and dressing.

Heat a large Dutch oven over medium-high heat and add oil. Season the pork shoulder with salt and pepper and sear until golden brown on all sides; remove the meat to a plate.

Add the apples, onion, and celery to the pan and sauté until translucent, about 3 minutes. Return the pork to the pan and add the white wine and apple juice; simmer for 1 minute. Add the stock, coriander and mustard seeds, and black peppercorns. Bring to a simmer, cover, and cook until meat is very tender, about 2 to 3 hours, adding more stock to cover the meat if needed.

Remove the pork from the pan, cover with foil, and let rest. Strain the braising liquid through a fine-mesh strainer into a medium bowl and discard the solids. Return the liquid to the pan and bring to a simmer; reduce by half. Stir the Dijon-style mustard into the braising sauce and simmer a few minutes; stir in the butter to gloss the sauce.

Toss the julienned apple with the whole-grain mustard. To serve, slice the pork, top with the sauce, and garnish with the apples.

2 tablespoons butter

3 garlic cloves, finely minced

2 cups sliced leeks, white and
    light green parts

2 tablespoons water

¾ pound chanterelle mushrooms,
    thinly sliced

½ cup dried cherries or cranberries,
    chopped

⅔ cup chopped pistachios, toasted

⅔ cup panko bread crumbs

Salt and pepper

4 (1-pound) baby chickens
    or a 3-pound fryer chicken,
    partially boned (see Note)

Extra virgin olive oil

½ cup chicken stock

Makes 4 servings

Chicken Stuffed
with Mushrooms,
Leeks, and Pistachios

DEVIL'S THUMB RANCH, TABERNASH & CHEF EVAN TREADWELL

For the very best flavor and texture, the ranch uses only pasture-raised baby chickens and stuffs them with chanterelle mushrooms. Substitute shiitake or crimini mushrooms if chanterelles are unavailable.

Melt the butter in a sauté pan over medium-low heat and add the garlic; cook just until fragrant, about 1 minute. Stir in the leeks and water and simmer, covered, over very low heat for 20 minutes, or until tender.

Add the mushrooms, stir, and cook until they release their juices. Continue cooking until all juices are reduced and concentrated so as to get the most flavor from the mushrooms. Stir in the dried cherries, pistachios, and bread crumbs and season with salt and pepper to taste.

Preheat the oven to 375 degrees. Season the inside of the chickens with salt and pepper. Divide the mushroom and leek mixture among the four baby chickens (or between the two halves of a larger chicken) and stuff. Reshape the chickens so that the filling is enclosed. Lay seam side down in a roasting pan, or truss with butcher's twine to hold together. Brush lightly with olive oil and season with salt and pepper. Bake, uncovered, until cooked through, about 45 minutes to an hour.

Remove the chickens from the roasting pan to a serving plate. Deglaze the pan by adding the chicken stock and gently scraping the bottom of the pan to pull up all the browned bits. Reduce liquid to a thin glaze and spoon over chicken before serving.

& *Note: If you are able to find baby chickens, ask your butcher to remove the back, rib, and thigh bones, leaving the flesh and skin intact. If you end up using a larger fryer chicken, ask the butcher to remove the backbone, cut the bird in half, and then remove the rib and thigh bones from each half. It may make stuffing the halves easier if you first gently pound out the breast meat slightly with a meat mallet.*

Shrimp

2 tablespoons chopped cilantro

1 tablespoon minced jalapeño

2 tablespoons lime juice

2 tablespoons lemon juice

1 teaspoon chili powder

1 tablespoon soy sauce

1 tablespoon brown sugar

2 teaspoons crushed
    red pepper flakes

1 cup extra virgin olive oil

1 ½ pounds of 16/20 (extra-large)
    shrimp, peeled and deveined

Salt and pepper

Cilantro and toasted macadamia
    nuts, for garnish (optional)

Rice

2 cups water

1 tablespoon butter

1 cup jasmine rice

2 tablespoons chopped cilantro

½ cup sweetened
    coconut flakes, toasted

½ cup coconut milk

Salt and pepper

Chile-Citrus Shrimp with Coconut Rice and Red Curry Vinaigrette

BLACKBELLY CATERING, BOULDER
FOUNDER/CHEF HOSEA ROSENBERG

*Blackbelly serves this flavorful Asian-inspired dish with Gingered Peas
(see recipe on page 53).*

For the shrimp:

Combine cilantro, jalapeño, lime juice, lemon juice, chili powder,
soy sauce, brown sugar, red pepper flakes, and olive oil in a medium
bowl and mix well. Add shrimp, toss to coat, and marinate in the
refrigerator overnight.

After preparing the rice and vinaigrette and just before serving,
remove the shrimp from the marinade and sauté in a large nonstick
skillet over medium–high heat until shrimp is pink, about 1 to 2
minutes per side; season with salt and pepper to taste.

For the rice:

Bring water to a boil in a medium saucepan. Add the butter and rice,
cover, and simmer until rice is just cooked, about 20 minutes. Toss
the rice with cilantro, coconut flakes, and coconut milk and season
with salt and pepper to taste.

(continued on page 96)

Vinaigrette

2 teaspoons red curry paste

3 tablespoons macadamia nut oil

2 teaspoons brown sugar

2 teaspoons orange juice

1 teaspoon lime juice

1 tablespoon red wine vinegar

2 teaspoons coconut milk

Makes 4 servings

For the vinaigrette:
Combine all ingredients in a small bowl and mix well.

Presentation:
Serve the shrimp on a bed of coconut rice and drizzle with red curry vinaigrette. Garnish with additional cilantro and toasted macadamia nuts.

Chile-Seasoned Pot-Roasted Pork

DUNTON HOT SPRINGS, DOLORES

Slow roasting pork as they do at the resort produces tender, juicy meat that falls apart with a fork. The chef serves the sliced meat topped with radishes and onions to create a riot of color on the plate.

1 (7-ounce) can chipotle chiles
    in adobo sauce

2 bay leaves, crushed

2 tablespoons cider vinegar

½ small white onion,
    roughly chopped

2 garlic cloves, roughly chopped

1 teaspoon dried marjoram,
    thyme, or oregano
    (or a mixture of dried herbs)

¼ teaspoon allspice

Pinch freshly ground cloves

1 cup water

1½ tablespoons canola oil
    (or rich-tasting lard if desired)

¼ to ½ teaspoon salt

3 pounds lean, boneless pork roast
    (shoulder or Boston butt)

8 romaine lettuce leaves, for garnish

3 radishes, thinly sliced, for garnish

2 thin slices white onion,
    broken into rings, for garnish

Makes 6 to 8 servings

Preheat the oven to 325 degrees. Combine the chiles (including the adobo sauce), bay leaves, vinegar, onion, garlic, herbs, allspice, cloves, and water in a blender and puree until smooth. Press through a medium-mesh strainer into a small bowl and discard solids.

Heat a 6-quart Dutch oven over medium-high heat and add the oil. When the oil is hot, add the chile puree. Stir constantly as the puree sears, concentrates, and darkens into a spicy-smelling paste, about 5 minutes. Remove from heat and season with salt to taste.

Cut the pork roast into slabs roughly 3 inches thick, making sure each slab is about the same thickness so they cook evenly. Lay the meat on the chile paste in the Dutch oven, and then turn the meat over to coat both sides with the paste.

Cover tightly and place in the preheated oven. Roast, basting the pork by turning the pieces in the chile paste every 30 minutes, until the meat is tender, about 2½ hours.

Remove from oven and let the pork stand, covered, for 20 to 30 minutes, to reabsorb juices before slicing

Presentation:
Line a platter with the lettuce leaves and use tongs to transfer the sliced meat to the platter. Sample the pan juices and add salt to taste; spoon the juices over the meat. Scatter the radishes and onion rings over the top to add color and texture.

  ❧ *Note: Depending on how much fat is in the pork roast, the juices may have more fat than you prefer. If so, simply pour the juices into a heat-safe glass measuring cup and allow the fat to rise to the top, then skim it off and discard. If the sauce is too thick, thin it with a bit of water.*

½ pound ground lamb

½ pound ground elk

½ pound ground pork

½ pound ground beef

½ cup finely chopped onions

¼ cup finely chopped carrots

¼ cup finely chopped celery

2 tablespoons dry mustard

1 ½ teaspoons salt

1 teaspoon pepper

2 cups fresh bread crumbs
     (see Note)

6 large eggs, beaten

2 tablespoons Tabasco sauce

1 pound sliced bacon

Makes 8 servings

While the Stanley Hotel,
located just a few miles from
Rocky Mountain National Park,
is listed on the National Register
of Historic Places, it may be best
known for inspiring Stephen King's
novel *The Shining*. Touted as one
of America's most haunted hotels,
the Stanley Hotel offers guests the
opportunity to take a ghost tour
while visiting.

Colorado Game Meatloaf

THE STANLEY HOTEL, ESTES PARK
EXECUTIVE CHEF RICHARD BEICHNER
FOOD AND BEVERAGE MANAGER MARK ORTELL

*A staple recipe for the Stanley Hotel, this meatloaf gives guests an
opportunity to experience some wild game introduced in a comfort-
food style. The bacon and eggs keep the game meats moist, and the
Tabasco adds nice background flavor.*

Preheat the oven to 325 degrees. Combine all the ground meats in
a large bowl and gently mix together. Add the onions, carrots, celery,
mustard, salt, pepper, and bread crumbs and gently mix until well
combined. Add the eggs and Tabasco and mix together.

Line a 9 x 5 x 3-inch loaf pan with slices of bacon across the bottom
and up all four sides. Place the meat mixture into the pan and top
with bacon slices. Bake until cooked through, about 1 hour.

Place the meatloaf under the broiler for a few minutes before serving
to crisp up the bacon on top. Transfer the meatloaf to a plate to
slice; remove uncrisp bacon from the sides and bottom before
serving, if desired.

❧ *Note: Fresh bread crumbs are easily made by roughly tearing fresh bread into
large chunks, then pulsing in a food processor until a fine crumb is formed.
Store any leftovers in the freezer.*

Lamb

1 whole leg of lamb, trimmed, with trimmings reserved for sauce

¼ cup chopped fresh rosemary

¼ cup extra virgin olive oil

Kosher salt

Pepper

Sauce

¼ cup extra virgin olive oil

Reserved lamb trimmings (or lamb neck bones)

½ cup sliced shallots

¼ cup sliced garlic

2 tomatoes, diced

1 tablespoon fresh thyme leaves

1 teaspoon black peppercorns

1 cup red wine

2 cups veal demi-glace (see Sources on page 154) or beef stock

Salt and pepper

Colorado Leg of Lamb with Creamy Polenta and Lamb Jus

JENNIFER JASINSKI, DENVER
EXECUTIVE CHEF AND OWNER OF RIOJA, BISTRO VENDOME, AND EUCLID HALL

Order a fresh leg of Colorado lamb from your butcher for this recipe, and ask him or her to debone it and clean the major muscles into separate pieces. Save the bones and trimmings to make a delicious sauce for the lamb. If you have purchased a boned leg of lamb, request some lamb neck bones to make the sauce.

For the lamb:
Season the leg of lamb with the rosemary, olive oil, and salt and pepper. Place in a baking dish and cover or in a sealed large plastic bag and marinate in the refrigerator for at least 1 hour or up to 1 day.

Grill the lamb to desired doneness—about 130 degrees internal temperature for medium rare—starting with the larger pieces so all the cuts finish cooking at the same time. Allow the lamb to rest for at least 5 minutes, wrapped in foil, before slicing into ¼-inch-thick pieces.

For the sauce:
While the lamb is marinating, heat a medium saucepan over medium-high heat and add the olive oil and reserved lamb trimmings to brown. Add the shallots and garlic and cook until golden. Stir in the tomatoes, thyme, peppercorns, red wine, and demi-glace. Bring the mixture to a simmer and cook, covered, for 30 minutes.

Strain the sauce through a fine-mesh strainer into a small bowl and discard solids. Return the sauce to a clean saucepan and bring to a light boil; cook until reduced by half, and then season with salt and pepper to taste. Keep the sauce warm until ready to serve. Lamb sauce may be made a day in advance and reheated.

(continued on page 100)

Polenta

5½ cups chicken or vegetable stock

1 cup coarse-ground polenta (not instant)

1 cup Haystack Mountain goat cheese (*see Sources on page 154*) or another high-quality goat cheese, crumbled

¾ cup crème fraîche

1 tablespoon chopped fresh thyme

Salt and pepper

Makes 8 servings

For the polenta:
While the lamb is cooking, add the stock to a large stockpot and bring to a simmer. Slowly whisk in the polenta and bring to a boil, stirring until the polenta begins to thicken. Reduce heat to very low and cook, stirring frequently to prevent burning, until the granules are tender, about 30 minutes to an hour.

When the polenta has finished cooking, remove the stockpot from the heat and stir in the goat cheese, crème fraîche, and thyme. Season with salt and pepper to taste. Cover and keep warm until ready to serve.

Presentation:
Spoon a ½ cup of the cooked polenta on each plate and lay fanned-out lamb slices over the polenta. Spoon the lamb sauce around and over the lamb and garnish with rosemary sprigs.

Mashed potatoes

2 Yukon gold potatoes,
    peeled and cubed

1 garlic clove, minced

2 tablespoons heavy cream

2 tablespoons butter

Salt and pepper

Elk

4 ounces granola, about 1 cup

2 tablespoons roasted garlic oil
    (see Note on page 102)

2 ounces bread crumbs

Olive oil, for searing chops

4 elk chops

Sauce

10 blackberries

4 ounces demi-glace
    (see Sources on page 154)

Makes 2 servings

Elk Chops with Blackberry Sauce and Garlic Mashers

HEARTHSTONE RESTAURANT, BRECKENRIDGE
MANAGING PARTNER RICHARD M. CARLETON
EXECUTIVE CHEF MICHAEL HALPIN

Breckenridge is not only a world-class ski resort, but a quaint little town that's loved by visitors and locals alike. The Hearthstone has been a fixture in the town for over twenty years and specializes in hand-cut steaks and game.

For the mashed potatoes:
Boil the potatoes until a knife easily slides out, about 15 to 25 minutes, and then drain. Mash with the garlic, cream, and butter and season with salt and pepper to taste.

For the elk:
Preheat the oven to 400 degrees. Combine the granola and roasted garlic oil in a small bowl and stir until the granola is evenly coated in oil. Place the granola and bread crumbs in a food processor and process until medium fine.

Heat a thin coating of olive oil in a large skillet over medium–high heat. Coat the elk chops with the granola mixture by gently pressing the mixture onto the chops and sear both sides until golden brown. Transfer the elk chops to a baking sheet and finish cooking in the oven for about 5 minutes for medium rare.

(continued on page 102)

With ten national monuments and recreation areas, twenty-six ski resorts, forty-six state and national parks, fifty-four mountains over 14,000 feet high, nearly 100 vineyards, and 300 days of sunshine each year, Colorado greets visitors with a seemingly endless variety of ways to enjoy their time outdoors in the Centennial State. Colorado ski resorts average nearly 300 inches of snow each year, yet they still boast an impressive 3,600 acres of snow-making capability. With a total of over 27,000 skiable acres, and twelve resorts ranked in the top thirty nationwide by *Ski Magazine*, Colorado is a popular destination for anyone serious about skiing or snowboarding.

For the sauce:
While the elk chops are in the oven, place the blackberries and demi-glace in a small saucepan and simmer just until berries are heated through.

Presentation:
Spoon the sauce onto individual plates and lay elk chops on top, with the garlic mashers alongside, or arrange as shown below.

☙ **Note:** *To make roasted garlic oil, simply simmer a couple of cloves of minced garlic in olive oil for about 20 minutes, taking care not to burn the garlic. Strain oil through a fine-mesh strainer into a small bowl and discard garlic. Alternatively, use the oil from making roasted garlic as outlined in the Guidelines for Recipes on page xviii.*

½ cup Ancho chili powder

½ cup espresso powder

¼ cup paprika

¼ cup brown sugar

2 tablespoons dry mustard

2 tablespoons salt

2 tablespoons pepper

2 tablespoons ground coriander

2 tablespoons oregano

1 tablespoon ground ginger

2 teaspoons chipotle chili powder

Extra virgin olive oil, for searing beef

1 (4-pound) beef tenderloin

Makes 8 servings

Espresso-Rubbed Beef Tenderloin

CAFÉ DIVA, STEAMBOAT SPRINGS ✷ CHEF KATE RENCH

This combination of chili powder and espresso creates an exciting rub for beef that Café Diva uses on whole beef tenderloin. You'll have plenty of rub left over, which may be saved for steaks and roasts.

Preheat the oven to 450 degrees. Combine Ancho chili powder, espresso powder, paprika, brown sugar, dry mustard, salt, pepper, coriander, oregano, ginger, and chipotle chili powder in a small bowl and mix well.

Heat a thin coating of olive oil in a large skillet over high heat and sear the beef on all sides until browned. Remove from heat and place the beef in a large bowl. Sprinkle with about ½ cup of the spice rub and coat evenly, adding more rub if needed.

Place the meat on a roasting rack over a baking sheet; roast the tenderloin until desired internal temperature, about 125 degrees for medium rare.

Remove from the oven and wrap the meat loosely in aluminum foil; let rest for 10 minutes before slicing and serving. Store extra rub in an airtight container until needed.

4 tablespoons butter, melted

1 teaspoon garlic powder

4 cups cubed baguette
 (1-inch cubes)

4 small new potatoes with
 skin intact, cubed

8 baby carrots with green tops intact

2 handfuls snow peas

8 asparagus spears

1 head cauliflower, cut into florets

½ cup milk

1½ cups dry white wine

Pinch white pepper

Pinch freshly grated nutmeg

11 ounces shredded fondue
 cheeses (see Notes)

2 tablespoons cornstarch

3 tablespoons water

Splash of Kirsch schnapps,
 such as Black Forest, or other
 high-quality brand (optional)

Chopped fresh rosemary, thyme,
 basil, or parsley

Makes 4 servings

Fondue

SONNENALP RESORT OF VAIL, VAIL
EXECUTIVE CHEF STEFAN SCHMID

*Fondue remains popular on the menu at the Swiss Chalet restaurant
at the Sonnenalp. You can vary the vegetables for dipping as you wish.*

Combine the butter and garlic powder; brush the baguette cubes
with garlic butter and toast under the broiler, turning once, so they
are golden brown on all sides. Steam the potatoes, carrots, snow
peas, and asparagus until softened but still crunchy. Cook the
cauliflower in a mixture of water and milk. Set the vegetables
and bread cubes aside.

Place a fondue pot on the stove over high heat. Pour in the wine
and add the white pepper and nutmeg. Bring to a simmer for a
few minutes for the raw alcohol to burn off.

Add the cheese and stir constantly in one direction so that the
cheese doesn't burn. Once the cheese is melted, mix the cornstarch
and water together in a small covered container; add the cornstarch
slurry to the cheese and simmer until the fondue is thick like
bubbling lava, about 1 to 2 minutes. If the fondue doesn't seem
thick enough, add more cornstarch slurry.

Just before serving, sauté the vegetables in garlic butter for one
minute and sprinkle with chopped herbs to taste. Add the Kirsch
schnapps to the fondue.

  Notes: *The Sonnenalp uses equal parts Appenzeller, Gruyère, and Freiburger
cheeses, but Ementhaller also works well. For variety, add chopped fresh herbs
(chives, rosemary, or parsley) to the cheese mixture just before serving; sauté
fresh morel or porcini mushrooms in a little butter with a few chopped shallots
and add them to the cheese; or substitute beer (like King Ludwig pilsner) for
the white wine.*

½ cup water

¼ cup sugar

4 cups water

1 cup slivered garlic
(sliced on garlic slicer or
mandoline or very thinly
with a knife)

1 tablespoon butter

4 tablespoons chopped
fresh sage leaves

4 chicken breast halves,
boneless with skin on

Salt and pepper

2 tablespoons canola oil

½ cup chicken stock

Makes 4 servings

Garlic and Sage-Stuffed Chicken Breasts

THE STEAMBOAT GRAND, STEAMBOAT SPRINGS
CHEF ERIC HYSLOP

Garlic is caramelized then combined with sage to create the unique stuffing for this chicken. At The Steamboat Grand, the dish is served with Lemon and Asparagus Risotto (see recipe on page 58).

Combine ½ cup water and sugar in a small saucepan over medium heat and bring to a gentle boil; reduce heat and simmer until syrup turns a light caramel color. While the simple syrup is cooking, bring 4 cups of water to a boil and blanch the slivered garlic for 8 minutes; drain and set aside.

When the simple syrup has reached a caramel color, turn the heat to low and add the butter, taking caution as butter can foam and boil over. When the butter has melted and the caramel has settled, add the garlic, turn the heat off, and let steep for 3 to 4 minutes. Pour the caramelized garlic onto a parchment-lined baking sheet, using a fork to spread the garlic out into a single layer. Allow the caramelized garlic to cool completely, then mix with the chopped sage.

Preheat oven to 350 degrees. Carefully make a pocket under the skin of each chicken breast and stuff with some of the garlic and sage mixture. Season the stuffed chicken breasts with salt and pepper. Heat the oil in an oven-safe sauté pan and sear the chicken breasts, skin side down, until golden brown. Turn the chicken breasts over and place entire sauté pan in the oven. Bake until the chicken is cooked through and the skin is crispy and lightly browned, about 20 to 30 minutes.

Remove the chicken and carefully wipe excess oil from the pan. Deglaze the hot pan by adding the chicken stock and gently scraping the bottom of the pan to pull up all the browned bits to create a simple, quick, and delicious pan sauce.

Shrimp

4 dried chiles (New Mexico,
  Guajillo, or Ancho)

2 dried Chile de Arbol chiles

1 (14-ounce) can tomatoes

1½ cups water

1 tablespoon canola oil

¼ medium onion, diced

3 garlic cloves, chopped

½ teaspoon cumin

½ teaspoon ground coriander

½ teaspoon Mexican oregano
  or other dried oregano

2 tablespoons chopped
  fresh cilantro

Juice of 1 lime
  (about 3 tablespoons)

1 teaspoon honey

1 teaspoon kosher salt

¼ teaspoon pepper

48 shrimp, 16/20 size
  (extra-large), peeled and
  deveined, with tail on

Salt and pepper

Grilled Shrimp with Tequila-Orange Sauce and Crispy Chorizo-Corn Relish

9545 RESTAURANT, THE INN AT LOST CREEK,
MOUNTAIN VILLAGE IN TELLURIDE
CHEF CHAD DILLON

Don't be put off by the long list of ingredients in this recipe; both the marinade and relish can be made the day before to save time.

For the shrimp:

Toast the chiles for 1 to 2 minutes over an open flame to bring out the aroma; let cool and remove seeds. Combine the chiles with the tomatoes and water in a medium saucepan over medium-high heat and bring to a boil. When the chiles have softened, puree in a traditional blender and then strain through a fine-mesh strainer into a large bowl; discard solids.

Meanwhile, heat the canola oil in a sauté pan and add the onion, garlic, cumin, coriander, oregano, cilantro, lime juice, honey, kosher salt, and pepper; cook until the onion is translucent and the garlic is aromatic, about 5 minutes.

Combine the chile puree and onion mixture in a medium saucepan over medium heat and simmer for 10 to 15 minutes; let cool. Add the shrimp and stir to coat; marinate for about 15 minutes. Remove shrimp and pat dry.

Sprinkle shrimp lightly with salt and pepper and grill over medium-high heat until just cooked through, about 1 to 2 minutes per side. Serve with chorizo-corn relish and spoon tequila-orange sauce over the shrimp.

Relish

2 ounces chorizo, diced small

1 cup cooked hominy,
    drained and rinsed

¼ cup diced red bell pepper

¼ cup dried sweet corn

2 tablespoons diced red onion

Juice of 1 lime
    (about 3 tablespoons)

2 tablespoons chopped cilantro

¼ teaspoon chipotle chili powder,
    or less to taste

2 teaspoons agave nectar

1 to 2 tablespoons canola oil

Salt and pepper

Sauce

2 teaspoons canola oil

1 teaspoon chopped garlic

1 teaspoon chopped shallot

¼ cup tequila

¼ cup orange juice

2 tablespoons lime juice

1 tablespoon agave nectar

¼ cup heavy cream

1 teaspoon orange zest

½ cup (1 stick) butter,
    cut into cubes

Salt and pepper

Makes 8 servings

For the relish:
Heat a skillet over medium-high heat, add the chorizo, and cook until the fat has rendered out. Combine the chorizo, rendered fat, hominy, bell pepper, corn, onion, lime juice, cilantro, chili powder, agave nectar, and oil and toss to combine; season with salt and pepper to taste.

For the sauce:
Heat canola oil in a small skillet over medium-high heat and sauté the garlic and shallot for 1 to 2 minutes. Deglaze the pan by adding the tequila and gently scraping the bottom of the pan; add the orange juice, lime juice, and agave nectar and reduce by half.

Remove from heat and stir in the cream and orange zest. Slowly stir in the butter, a few cubes at a time, whisking constantly until the sauce is fully emulsified; season with salt and pepper to taste.

Schnitzel

8 (3-ounce) medallions of veal eye
    round, pounded very thin

Flour, for dredging

Canola oil, for frying

Chopped fresh parsley,
    for garnish (optional)

Mushroom sauce

½ cup (1 stick) butter

1 large yellow onion, diced

2 pounds of a variety of mushrooms
    (white button, chanterelle,
    porcini, morel, or wild forest
    mushrooms), quartered or sliced

½ cup white wine

½ to 1 cup heavy cream

Salt and pepper

1 bay leaf

½ teaspoon ground nutmeg

1 teaspoon mushroom base,
    for depth of flavor (optional)

Chopped fresh parsley,
    for garnish (optional)

Makes 4 servings

Jaeger Schnitzel with Wild Mushroom Sauce

PEPI'S RESTAURANT, HOTEL GASTHOF GRAMSHAMMER, VAIL
HELMUT KASCHITZ

You'll feel just as if you're dining in the Swiss Alps when eating this classic Old World recipe. The schnitzel could be prepared with chicken breasts pounded very thin in lieu of the veal.

For the schnitzel:
Dredge veal medallions in a bit of flour. Heat 1 to 2 tablespoons of oil in a large sauté pan over medium-high heat and cook the veal medallions until they are nicely browned on both sides. Work in batches, adding more oil as needed, until all the medallions are cooked. Serve with a ladle of mushroom sauce over the veal and sprinkle with chopped parsley.

For the mushroom sauce:
Heat the butter in a large skillet over medium-high heat and sauté the onions until they are softened and slightly golden. Add the mushrooms and cook until the mushrooms have released all their juices and begun to caramelize. Add the white wine and cook until reduced by half.

Pour in enough heavy cream to cover the mushrooms and season with salt and pepper to taste. Add the bay leaf, nutmeg, and mushroom base and simmer just until slightly thickened. Remove the bay leaf and add chopped fresh parsley just before serving.

After the 10th Mountain Division trained here in World War II, two veterans returned and opened the resort of Vail in 1962, marking the beginning of what is now a world-famous resort town. Today Vail is home to the largest single-mountain ski resort in the United States, surrounded by a charming town that is strikingly similar to a village in the Swiss Alps. Resorts like the Sonnenalp and Hotel Gasthof Gramshammer help promote the fairy tale by serving authentic Old World foods like fondue and schnitzel.

Burgers

8 ounces ground lamb

1 teaspoon chopped fresh rosemary
    or thyme

1 ounce fresh chopped mint

¼ teaspoon salt

⅛ teaspoon pepper

8 mini burger buns

Chutney

1 tablespoon canola oil

½ pound Roma tomatoes
    (about 3 tomatoes),
    roughly chopped

2 tablespoons minced fresh ginger

½ white onion, finely chopped

¼ cup red wine vinegar

¼ cup sugar

Makes 2 to 4 servings

Lamb Slider with Mint and Tomato-Ginger Chutney

THE STANLEY HOTEL, ESTES PARK
EXECUTIVE CHEF RICHARD BEICHNER
FOOD AND BEVERAGE MANAGER MARK ORTELL

*This recipe pays homage to one of the chef's favorite late-night meals—
a mini burger that beckons you late at night to satisfy the hunger in
your belly before you hit the sack.*

For the burgers:
Combine ground lamb, rosemary, mint, salt, and pepper in a small
bowl and mix well. Shape into eight small burgers. Grill or pan sear
to desired doneness and place each burger in a mini bun. Top with
tomato–ginger chutney.

For the chutney:
Combine all ingredients in a nonreactive saucepan, such as stainless
steel, and cook over low heat until all ingredients have broken down
and formed a thick sauce, about 1 hour. Chill before serving. Chutney
may be stored in the refrigerator for up to 2 weeks.

2 (1½-pound) live lobsters

2 cups canola oil

1 tablespoon paprika

12 ounces elbow macaroni

½ cup white wine

½ cup white wine vinegar

1 tablespoon black peppercorns

1 large shallot, sliced

½ cup heavy cream

1½ cups (3 sticks) butter,
    cut into cubes

½ cup (1 stick) butter

8 ounces mascarpone cheese

Salt and white pepper

Chervil, for garnish (optional)

Makes 4 servings

❧ **Note:** *This recipe is best when made
with fresh lobster. If you are unsure
how to dispatch a live lobster with
a knife, ask your local fishmonger
to explain the procedure.*

Lobster Mac and Cheese

MIZUNA, DENVER   ❧   CHEF FRANK BONANNO

*This dish is perhaps the most decadent in the entire cookbook. With a rich
butter-based sauce and lobster meat, it's a great choice for a special celebration.
If you'd like to make it slightly less decadent, cut the ingredients for the sauce
in half and reduce the pasta to 8 ounces.*

Heat a large pot of salted water over high heat until boiling. While waiting
for water to boil, dispatch the lobsters with a knife (*see Note*) and remove
the tails and claws. When the water comes to a boil, turn off the heat,
add the tails and claws, and cover. Let the tails sit in the boiling water for
6 minutes, then remove and plunge them into an ice bath. After another
2 minutes, remove the claws and plunge them into the ice bath. When the
lobster parts are cool, remove the meat from the shells, reserving the shells.
Chop the meat into large pieces and refrigerate until ready to use.

Place the lobster bodies and reserved shells in a pot and cover with 2 cups
of oil. Heat until nearly boiling, then turn off the heat and let sit for 10
minutes. Add the paprika and let rest for 30 minutes. Strain through a
fine-mesh strainer into a bowl, discard solids, and set the oil aside.

While the lobster is resting, boil the macaroni in salted water until al dente
(an extra-firm bite); test often as brands vary in cooking time. Drain and
set aside.

Place the white wine, vinegar, peppercorns, and shallot in a nonreactive
pan, such as stainless steel, over medium heat and simmer until nearly dry.
Add the heavy cream and reduce by two-thirds.

Slowly whisk in the 1½ cups of cubed butter, one piece at a time, until
fully emulsified. Strain through a fine-mesh strainer into a medium bowl,
discard solids, and set the bowl over another bowl of warm water to
hold the sauce warm until ready to use.

Melt the ½ cup of butter in a large saucepan over medium heat and
add the mascarpone, stirring until melted. Add the cooked lobster, stir,
and heat until warm. Add the cooked pasta and heat until just warmed
through. Stir in the wine sauce and season with salt and white pepper
to taste. Divide evenly among four serving bowls; garnish with chervil
and drizzle with the reserved lobster oil.

1 quart heavy cream

2 (14-ounce) cans chicken stock

1 pound Nueske's smoked chicken
    or other high-quality brand

8 ounces elbow macaroni

4 ounces Avalanche goat cheese
    or other high-quality brand

6 tablespoons flour

4 tablespoons butter

¼ cup chopped fresh parsley

Salt and pepper

Makes 4 servings

Mountain High Mac and Cheese

ST. REGIS HOTEL, ASPEN   ❧   EXECUTIVE CHEF JASON ADAMS

The highlight of this simple macaroni and cheese recipe is the addition of smoked chicken. If you can't find a whole Nueske's smoked chicken (see Sources on page 154), buy a large piece of smoked chicken from the deli and shred it to use in the recipe.

Combine the heavy cream and chicken stock in a medium stock-pot over medium heat and simmer until reduced by half, about 45 minutes.

While the mixture is reducing, shred the smoked chicken and set aside. Cook the macaroni in salted boiling water until al dente (an extra-firm bite); drain and set aside.

Whisk the goat cheese into the reduced cream mixture. Heat the flour and butter together in a large stockpot over medium-high heat, stirring constantly as the butter melts, then whisk in the cream mixture a little at a time to form the cheese sauce. If needed, strain through a fine-mesh strainer into a medium bowl to remove any lumps.

Add the cooked macaroni and the chicken to the cheese sauce and stir until well combined. Stir in the parsley and season with salt and pepper to taste.

¼ cup canola oil

½ cup finely diced onions

2 garlic cloves, minced

2 tablespoons flour

1 cup hot chicken stock

1½ cups diced roasted mild
    green chile peppers
    (may use canned)

1 tomato, diced

1 teaspoon ground coriander

1 tablespoon chopped fresh cilantro

Salt and pepper

Tabasco sauce

6 small New York strip steaks

Makes 6 servings

New York Strip Steaks with Gonzales Sauce

NORTH FORK RANCH, SHAWNEE & OWNER KAREN S. MAY

An easy-to-make sauce based on roasted green chiles enhances steaks for diners at the North Fork Ranch. If using fresh-roasted chiles, be sure to assess the chiles' heat level prior to proceeding with the recipe.

Heat the oil in a medium saucepan over medium-high heat and sauté the onions and garlic until tender, about 5 minutes. Whisk in the flour and cook for 3 minutes. Slowly whisk in the stock and continue whisking until sauce thickens, about 5 minutes. Add the chile peppers, tomato, coriander, and cilantro and stir together. Reduce heat to simmer and cook for 20 minutes; season with salt and Tabasco sauce to taste.

Season steaks with salt and pepper and grill to desired doneness. Let meat rest a few minutes before serving with Gonzales sauce.

4 tablespoons butter

1 pound chanterelle mushrooms, quartered

2 shallots, minced

6 garlic cloves, minced

8 ounces vermouth

3 cups heavy cream

1 teaspoon minced fresh tarragon

1 teaspoon minced fresh chervil

1 teaspoon minced fresh flat-leaf parsley

1 teaspoon minced fresh chives

Kosher salt

White pepper

8 (6-ounce) Colorado striped bass fillets, skin on, or other mild whitefish

2 tablespoons canola oil

Makes 8 servings

Pan-Roasted Colorado Striped Bass with Chanterelle Mushroom Vin Blanc

LA TOUR, VAIL   &   CHEF/PROPRIETOR PAUL FERZACCA

La Tour serves modern French-American cuisine in the heart of Vail, and local residents have voted it the best restaurant in Vail for the past five years. If you can't find Colorado striped bass (see Sources on page 154) for this recipe, substitute another mild whitefish.

Heat a 2-quart saucepan over medium–high heat and add the butter. Sauté the chanterelles until they are slightly golden brown, then add the shallots and garlic and cook until shallots are translucent. Deglaze the pan by adding the vermouth and gently scraping the bottom of the pan; reduce liquid by three-quarters.

Add the heavy cream and stir until well blended; bring to a simmer and reduce by half, so that the cream coats the back of a spoon. Stir in the tarragon, chervil, parsley, and chives and season with salt and white pepper to taste. Keep sauce warm until ready to serve.

Pat the fish dry with a paper towel and season with salt and white pepper. Heat a large nonstick sauté pan over high heat and add the canola oil. Place the bass in the pan skin side down and cook about 4 minutes, or until skin is as crispy as possible. Turn the fillets over and cook another 1 to 2 minutes. Serve the fish skin side up on a bed of the chanterelle mushroom sauce.

& **Note:** *If chervil is unavailable, double the quantity of tarragon.*

1 rack pork spareribs
(about 2 pounds)

Salt and pepper

3 medium peaches,
peeled and diced

1 cup ketchup

1 tablespoon cider vinegar

1 tablespoon Worcestershire sauce

1 teaspoon prepared mustard

¼ cup brown sugar

2 tablespoons minced fresh
rosemary

1 teaspoon salt

½ teaspoon pepper

Makes 2 to 4 servings

Peach BBQ Pork Spareribs

Peach trees can be found all over the Denver metro area, and I created this easy barbecue sauce after a bumper crop of peaches from the trees in my own yard. The peaches pair beautifully with the pork, and you may use fresh, canned, or frozen peaches for the sauce.

Preheat the oven to 400 degrees. Season ribs with salt and pepper. Line the bottom of a broiler pan or roasting pan with aluminum foil and lay the ribs on the foil; roast for 20 minutes to sear the ribs.

While ribs are roasting, combine the peaches, ketchup, vinegar, Worcestershire sauce, mustard, brown sugar, rosemary, salt, and pepper in a food processor; pulse to combine, then whirl until smooth.

Remove ribs from the oven and cover with sauce. Seal the entire pan tightly with aluminum foil and return ribs to the oven. Reduce heat to 250 degrees and cook for 3 hours. Ribs may be made up to this point the day before.

Remove the foil, increase the temperature to 350 degrees, and return ribs to oven to cook until nicely caramelized and the meat falls from the bone, about 1 hour.

8 large Portobello mushroom caps,
gills removed

Extra virgin olive oil

Salt and pepper

2 tablespoons fresh thyme leaves

1 cup balsamic vinegar

1 cup water

½ cup Gorgonzola cheese crumbles

Aioli or regular mayonnaise

8 sandwich rolls or sliced focaccia

¼ cup chopped walnuts

Makes 8 servings

Portobello Mushroom Burger

BEAUMONT HOTEL & SPA, OURAY
EXECUTIVE CHEF CHARLIE BARTOSEK

The town of Ouray is nestled in a small valley below some of the most breathtaking, towering peaks of the Rocky Mountains. With one glance down the valley, visitors come to understand why it's nicknamed the Switzerland of America.

Preheat the oven to 350 degrees. Place the mushrooms on a baking sheet, top side down. Drizzle olive oil, sprinkle salt and pepper, and spread thyme over caps. Combine the vinegar and water and pour over caps; cover with aluminum foil and bake for 20 minutes. Remove the caps and discard the cooking liquid.

Lay the mushrooms top side down on a rimmed baking sheet and top with Gorgonzola; place under the broiler for 1 to 2 minutes to melt the cheese. Spread sandwich rolls with aioli or mayonnaise and place one mushroom cap on each roll. Top with walnuts and serve.

(see photograph on page 91)

The Beaumont Hotel opened in 1887 during the gold boom and has a long history of hosting important guests–from Presidents Theodore Roosevelt and Herbert Hoover to actresses Sarah Bernhardt and Angie Dickenson to modern-day icons like Oprah Winfrey. With declining tourism, the hotel closed in 1964 and sat dilapidated until it was bought in 1998 and lovingly restored over the next five years. With a grand reopening in 2003, it was awarded one of the first four Preserve America Presidential Awards for historic preservation.

Gratin

1 tablespoon extra virgin olive oil

4 heads of fennel, julienned

2 shallots, julienned

1 cup heavy cream

½ cup grated Parmigiano-Reggiano cheese

½ teaspoon nutmeg

½ cup fresh bread crumbs

2 tablespoons finely chopped tarragon

Extra virgin olive oil

Beurre blanc

1 shallot, diced

¼ cup white wine

¼ cup white wine vinegar

10 peppercorns

1 bay leaf

1 tablespoon lemon juice

Juice of 4 blood or navel oranges (about 1 cup)

½ cup (1 stick) butter, cut into small cubes

Prosciutto-Wrapped Scallops with Fennel Gratin and Blood Orange Beurre Blanc

LUCA D'ITALIA, DENVER ❦ CHEF FRANK BONANNO

The cuisine at Luca reflects the chef's upbringing in a family home where the aromas from the pastas of his Sicilian grandmothers filled the kitchen, while he and his mother tried out recipes from Julia Child. The restaurant is named for his son Luca, whose picture can be found on the dining room wall.

For the gratin:

Preheat the oven to 400 degrees and grease an 8 x 8 x 2-inch baking dish. Heat the oil in a large skillet over medium heat and add fennel and shallots. Sweat until tender, about 10 minutes, but do not brown. Remove from heat and place the onions in a small mixing bowl. Add the heavy cream, cheese, and nutmeg and mix well.

Pour the fennel mixture into the prepared baking dish. Toss the bread crumbs with the tarragon and spread over the top of the fennel. Drizzle with a little olive oil and bake until the top is golden brown and the cream has thickened, about 30 minutes. Let cool for a few minutes before cutting to serve.

For the beurre blanc:

While the gratin is baking, combine the shallot, white wine, vinegar, peppercorns, bay leaf, and lemon juice in a small nonreactive sauce-pan, such as stainless steel. Simmer over medium heat until almost dry, and then add the blood orange juice. Simmer until reduced by two-thirds.

(continued on page 118)

Scallops

16 dry-pack scallops, U10 size

16 pieces paper-thin
  Prosciutto di Parma

Salt and white pepper

3 tablespoons extra virgin olive oil

2 tablespoons basil oil (optional)

4 cups fresh mâche, or other
  baby green lettuce

Extra virgin olive oil, for dressing

Lemon juice, for dressing

Makes 4 servings

Reduce heat to low and whisk in the butter, one piece at a time, until all the butter is emulsified. Strain through a fine–mesh strainer into a small bowl, discard solids, and hold sauce in a warm spot to prevent the sauce from separating.

For the scallops:
Wrap a piece of prosciutto around each scallop and season lightly with salt and white pepper. Heat a large sauté pan over high heat and, when very hot, add 1 to 2 tablespoons of olive oil. Sear half of the scallops on one side until golden brown, and then flip and continue cooking, for a total of about 5 minutes for both sides. Remove to a paper towel and cook the remaining scallops, adding oil if needed.

Cut the fennel gratin into four pieces and place in the center of each plate. Place four scallops around the gratin and drizzle with the buerre blanc and a little basil oil. Dress the mâche with olive oil and lemon juice and place on top of the gratin.

2 pork tenderloins

Extra virgin olive oil

Chipotle chili powder

16 ounces frozen raspberries

2 tablespoons raspberry jam

¼ cup chicken stock

¼ cup orange juice

½ teaspoon onion salt

¼ teaspoon pepper

1 tablespoon cornstarch

Makes 6 servings

Raspberry-Chipotle Pork Tenderloin

NORTH FORK RANCH, SHAWNEE   &   OWNER KAREN S. MAY

To keep pork tenderloin moist and juicy, don't cook it past 145 to 150 degrees internal temperature. Since chipotle seasoning can be quite hot, use it sparingly unless you know you love spicy foods.

Rub the pork with olive oil and sprinkle very lightly with chipotle seasoning. Heat grill to medium high or preheat oven to 375 degrees; grill or roast until internal temperature is 145 to 150 degrees, about 30 to 40 minutes. Let meat rest before slicing.

Combine raspberries, jam, stock, orange juice, onion salt, pepper, and cornstarch in a medium saucepan over medium-high heat and bring to a boil. Reduce heat and simmer for 10 minutes.

Slice cooked pork and serve with sauce.

2 tablespoons extra virgin olive oil

4 (6-ounce) bone-in lamb chops

Salt and pepper

½ cup heavy cream

2 (14-ounce) cans white beans
    (cannellini)

2 roasted red peppers,
    peeled and diced small

1 (15-ounce) can artichoke hearts,
    drained and roughly chopped

1 cup lamb sauce or demi-glace
    (see Note)

1 tablespoon chopped tarragon

20 roasted garlic cloves,
    whole or pureed smooth

Fresh rosemary or thyme,
    for garnish (optional)

Makes 4 servings

Roast Colorado Lamb Chops with White Beans and Tarragon-Garlic Sauce

RESTAURANT KEVIN TAYLOR, HOTEL TEATRO, DENVER
EXECUTIVE CHEF KEVIN TAYLOR

Restaurant Kevin Taylor has received the AAA Four Diamond Award, the Mobil Travel Guide Four Star Award, and the Wine Spectator "Best of" Award of Excellence, making it one of the most highly recognized restaurants in Colorado.

Preheat the oven to 400 degrees. Heat the oil in a large skillet over medium–high heat. Season the lamb chops with salt and pepper and sear on both sides until golden brown. Transfer lamb chops to a baking sheet and finish cooking in the oven, about 3 to 5 minutes for medium rare.

Combine the heavy cream and white beans in a small sauté pan and heat over high heat until the cream begins to simmer; gently stir in the red peppers and artichoke hearts and season with salt and pepper to taste. Combine the lamb sauce and tarragon in a small saucepan over medium heat and bring just to a simmer.

Presentation:
Spoon the white bean mixture in the center of four plates and top each with a lamb chop. Spoon the lamb sauce around the plate and garnish with roasted garlic cloves or a few dots of roasted garlic puree. Finish by garnishing with fresh herbs.

⤙ *Note: Refer to the Colorado Leg of Lamb recipe from Jennifer Jasinski on page 99 for a recipe for lamb sauce.*

1 (15-ounce) can quartered
   artichoke hearts, drained

¼ cup pitted Kalamata olives

¼ cup pitted Manzanilla olives

3 Roma tomatoes, seeded
   and diced

2 tablespoons thinly sliced
   fresh basil leaves

1 tablespoon extra virgin olive oil

Juice of ½ a small lemon
   (about 1½ tablespoons)

Salt and pepper

1 to 2 tablespoons extra virgin
   olive oil

4 (6-ounce) salmon fillets

Makes 4 servings

Salmon with Artichoke, Tomato, and Olive Tapenade

HOTEL BOULDERADO, BOULDER
EXECUTIVE CHEF PETER M. MORRISON

In 1909, in an effort to spur growth, a civic organization in Boulder sold stock to raise funds to build a first-class hotel that would attract tourists. The name chosen combined both Boulder and Colorado so that guests would never forget where they had stayed. Over 100 years later, the Hotel Boulderado still welcomes guests.

Slice the quartered artichoke hearts lengthwise and place in a small mixing bowl. Cut the olives lengthwise into quarters and add to the bowl, along with the tomatoes, basil, 1 tablespoon olive oil, and lemon juice; stir gently to combine and season with salt and pepper to taste.

Season salmon fillets with salt and pepper. Heat 1 to 2 tablespoons olive oil in a large nonstick skillet over medium–high heat and add the fillets, flesh side down. Cook until golden brown, about 3 to 5 minutes, then flip, reduce heat, and continue to cook until desired internal temperature, about 3 minutes for medium well.

Serve salmon with tapenade on top.

4 boneless chicken breasts, skin on

Salt and pepper

3 red bell peppers,
    roughly chopped

1 pint orange juice

½ teaspoon crushed
    red pepper flakes

2 tablespoons apple cider vinegar

3 artichoke hearts, diced into
    ¼-inch pieces

1 large carrot, diced into
    ¼-inch pieces

1 onion, diced into ¼-inch pieces

2 celery stalks, diced into
    ¼-inch pieces

Juice of 1 lemon
    (about 3 tablespoons)

1 cup white wine

1 cup water

7 tablespoons butter, divided

2 bay leaves

3 tablespoons extra virgin olive oil

Makes 4 servings

Slow-Poached Chicken with Red Pepper-Citrus Sauce and Stewed Artichoke

OPUS, LITTLETON   ℚ   CHEF SEAN MCGAUGHEY

The chef at Opus uses a poaching technique to create a succulent and tender breast of chicken that is pretty when sliced. If you prefer to skip this step, simply pan sear, grill, or roast your chicken breasts and proceed with the recipe.

Season chicken breasts with salt and pepper and roll tightly into a log shape, skin side out. Wrap tightly in several layers of plastic wrap, tying each end securely with butcher's twine. Refrigerate for 2 hours.

Heat a large pot of water and use a candy or frying thermometer to constantly measure the temperature at a consistent 140 to 150 degrees, which is usually just below simmering. Add the plastic-wrapped chicken and slowly poach for 2 hours, weighing down the breasts with a lid or plate as needed to keep them fully submerged. Remove chicken and chill in an ice bath until completely cooled.

While the chicken is cooling, prepare the sauce. Combine peppers, orange juice, red pepper flakes, and vinegar in a medium saucepan and cook, uncovered, over medium heat until the peppers are tender and liquid is reduced by half. While still warm, puree the mixture in a blender until smooth and season with salt to taste. If you desire a smoother texture, as they do at Opus, strain the sauce through a fine-mesh strainer into a small bowl and discard solids.

Combine the artichokes, carrot, onion, celery, lemon juice, white wine, water, 6 tablespoons of the butter, and bay leaves in a medium saucepan over medium heat and cook until vegetables are tender and the cooking liquid is reduced and slightly thickened. If vegetables are not tender by the time the cooking liquid is evaporated, add more water and cook down until you reach desired tenderness. Cover to keep warm while you finish the chicken.

To finish preparing the chicken, heat the olive oil in a large skillet over medium–high heat. Remove chicken from the plastic wrap and sear until skin is crispy and golden brown on all sides, about 5 to 10 minutes. Just before removing from pan, add remaining 1 tablespoon of butter and baste the chicken for 1 minute with melted butter. Remove chicken and let rest before slicing.

Presentation:
Spoon pepper sauce in the middle of the plate. Slice chicken in ½-inch slices, place in the center of the sauce, and top with braised vegetables.

Crab cakes

2 pounds crab meat

½ cup finely diced red onion

1 tablespoon minced garlic

2 poblano peppers, diced small

1 jalapeño, diced small

2 cups mayonnaise

1 ½ tablespoons Southwest
   seasoning *(see page 126)*

1 ½ tablespoons Old Bay seasoning

3 large eggs

2 cups panko bread crumbs

Flour, for dredging (optional)

Eggs, beaten, for dipping (optional)

Bread crumbs, for coating (optional)

Canola oil, for frying

Sauce

¾ cup roasted red peppers
   (about 3 small peppers)

2 garlic cloves, minced

¼ cup fresh dill

1 tablespoon capers

½ cup pickle relish

4 dashes Tabasco sauce

Juice of ½ small lemon
   (about 1 ½ tablespoons)

1 cup mayonnaise

Salt and pepper

Southwestern Crab Cakes

MAHOGANY GRILLE, THE STRATER HOTEL, DURANGO
CHEF DAVID CUNTZ

This recipe produces a large batch of crab cakes, which is perfect for a party. To partially prepare ahead, the crab cakes may be frozen, unbreaded and uncooked, and wrapped well in plastic wrap. Thaw completely in the refrigerator before proceeding with the recipe.

For the crab cakes:

Combine the crab, onion, garlic, peppers, and jalapeño in a large bowl. Place the mayonnaise in a small bowl. Combine the Southwest and Old Bay seasonings in a separate bowl; add the seasonings to the mayonnaise and stir until well mixed.

Using a fork, stir the mayonnaise and eggs into the crab mixture, then stir in the panko bread crumbs. Refrigerate for 10 minutes.

Scoop crab mixture into scant ⅓-cup portions and mold into twenty crab cakes. If you desire a breaded crust, dredge each cake in a little flour, dip into beaten eggs, and then coat in bread crumbs.

Preheat the oven to 350 degrees. Heat about ¼ inch of canola oil in a large skillet over medium heat and, working in batches, fry the crab cakes until golden brown on each side. Make sure that the oil comes up halfway on the cakes so the sides brown as well, adding more oil as needed while cooking.

Place the crab cakes on a baking sheet and bake for 10 minutes. Serve with roasted red pepper tartar sauce.

(continued on page 126)

Southwest seasoning

2 tablespoons chili powder

2 tablespoons paprika

1 tablespoon ground coriander

1 tablespoon garlic powder

1 tablespoon salt

1 tablespoon cumin

1 teaspoon cayenne pepper

1 teaspoon crushed
    red pepper flakes

1 teaspoon dried oregano

Yields 20 large crab cakes

For the sauce:
Add the peppers, garlic, dill, capers, relish, Tabasco, and lemon juice to a food processor and pulse until chopped small. Add the mayonnaise and continue to pulse until incorporated; season with salt and pepper to taste.

For the Southwest seasoning:
Mix all the spices together and store in a covered container. Seasoning may also be used on chicken, fish, steak, or vegetables, or stirred into butter.

The Strater Hotel was built in 1887 by Henry Strater, who, although underage and without money of his own, was able to borrow money to fund the hotel's construction. In later years, Western author Louis L'Amour stayed at the Strater, in a room above the Diamond Belle Saloon, because he felt the honky-tonk music helped set the mood for his novels of the Old West.

1 celery stalk, roughly chopped

1 carrot, roughly chopped

½ yellow onion, roughly chopped

3 garlic cloves, roughly chopped

2 tablespoons extra virgin olive oil

2½ pounds ground lamb

¼ cup tomato paste

1 (28-ounce) can crushed tomatoes

2 teaspoons kosher salt

1½ teaspoons paprika

½ teaspoon crushed
    red pepper flakes

½ teaspoon pepper

1 pound spaghetti (or other
    pasta of choice)

Makes 8 servings

Spaghetti with Braised Lamb Sugo

THE STEAMBOAT GRAND, STEAMBOAT SPRINGS
CHEF ERIC HYSLOP

A traditional spaghetti sauce takes on new interest when it's made with lamb instead of ground beef, and the result is a perfect entrée after a full day of skiing. If you don't have a food processor, be sure to very finely mince the vegetables before making the sugo.

Add the celery, carrot, onion, and garlic to a food processor and puree until finely chopped. Heat a large stockpot over medium-high heat and add the olive oil. Add the pureed vegetables and sauté for 10 minutes. Add the ground lamb and cook for 5 minutes, or until just starting to turn brown. Add the tomato paste and stir to incorporate. Stir in crushed tomatoes and all the juices, cover, and lower heat to a simmer; cook for 2 hours, skimming fat and juices often.

Heat a large stockpot of salted water to boiling over high heat; add the spaghetti and cook until al dente; drain and set aside.

Add the salt, paprika, red pepper flakes, and black pepper to the sauce and stir to combine. Serve lamb sugo over cooked spaghetti.

Spinach Florentine-Stuffed Trout

CASTLE MARNE BED AND BREAKFAST, DENVER
MELISSA FEHER-PEIKER

Trout, one of the few fish that are local to Colorado, is popular for sport fishing in the state. The spinach stuffing used at Castle Marne goes perfectly with the delicate flavor of the fish.

2 tablespoons butter

2 tablespoons flour

½ cup chopped onion

½ cup chicken stock

½ cup milk

1 (10-ounce) package of frozen spinach, thawed and squeezed dry

1 tablespoon grated Parmesan cheese

Salt and pepper

2 small trout (about ½ pound each), cleaned and deboned

Butter

2 lemons

Makes 2 servings

Preheat the oven to 350 degrees. Melt the butter in a medium sauce-pan and stir in the flour; cook for 1 minute. Add the onion, stir, and cook for another minute. Slowly whisk in the stock and milk, stirring until thickened.

Add the spinach and stir until well mixed; continue cooking over low heat, stirring constantly, for about 5 minutes. Stir in the Parmesan cheese and season with salt and pepper to taste.

Spray a 13 x 9 x 2-inch glass baking dish with cooking spray and lay the trout fillets in the dish. Spoon an equal amount of the spin-ach mixture in the cavities of the two fish and gently fold closed. Top each fish with a few small pieces of butter. Cut 1 lemon in half and squeeze the juice from half of the lemon over the top. Slice the remaining half of the lemon and place the lemon slices on the fish. Bake, uncovered, until cooked through, about 20 minutes. Slice the second lemon into wedges; serve fish with fresh lemon wedges.

2 tablespoons extra virgin olive oil

1 cup finely diced white onion

1 cup finely diced celery

1 cup finely diced leeks

1 pound ground beef

1 pound ground veal

1 pound ground pork

Salt and pepper

1 cup veal or chicken stock

3 cups whole milk

3 cups heavy cream

Pieces of Parmigiano-Reggiano rinds

1 ½ pounds Tagliatelle pasta
(fresh if possible)

Minced fresh sage, for garnish

Minced fresh rosemary, for garnish

Parmigiano-Reggiano cheese,
shaved for topping pasta

Makes 10 to 12 servings

Tagliatelle Pasta with White Bolognese

BAROLO GRILL, DENVER
OWNER BLAIR TAYLOR   EXECUTIVE CHEF DARREL TRUETT

As the owner of Barolo Grill, Blair Taylor is so intent on making sure his staff understands and appreciates the food of Italy that he takes them on a culinary trip to Italy every year. This creamy meat sauce is a nice alternative to a traditional red Bolognese sauce.

Heat the olive oil in a large saucepan over medium–high heat and add the onion, celery, and leeks; sauté until vegetables are translucent, about 5 minutes.

Add the ground beef, veal, and pork and cook until no longer pink. Season with salt and pepper and deglaze pan by adding the stock and gently scraping the bottom of the pan to pull up all the browned bits; simmer for 2 minutes.

Add milk, cream, and cheese rinds and bring to a simmer; cook, uncovered, stirring occasionally, until the sauce reduces and thickens, about 1 to 2 hours. Remove cheese rinds when done.

Cook pasta in salted boiling water until al dente (an extra–firm bite) and drain. Toss together pasta and Bolognese sauce in a large sauté pan. Add the desired amount of sage and rosemary to flavor. Garnish with shaved Parmigiano–Reggiano cheese and serve immediately.

1 (3½-pound) pork shoulder or butt

10 cups water

1 medium onion, quartered

3 garlic cloves, minced

1 tablespoon salt

40 dry cornhusks

10 Guajillo chiles or dried
    New Mexico or Ancho chiles,
    stems removed

6 cups Maseca corn flour or other
    high-quality corn flour

¾ cup lard or vegetable shortening

1½ teaspoons baking powder

2 teaspoons salt

Yields 40 tamales

Traditional Home-Style Red Chile Pork Tamales

MEZCAL, DENVER   ❧   CHEF ROBERTO DIAZ

Chef Roberto Diaz demonstrated his tamales to a crowd at the annual Cherry Creek Art Festival, explaining how his family prepared them in his native Mexico. Serve tamales with traditional condiments such as guacamole, salsa, sour cream, lime wedges, and chopped cilantro. Leftovers freeze well.

Place the pork in a large stockpot with the water, onion, garlic, and salt and bring to a boil. Simmer, covered, until the meat is very tender, about 2 to 4 hours.

Remove the meat from the broth and allow both to cool. When meat is cool, shred using two forks. Strain the broth through a fine-mesh strainer over a large bowl and discard solids.

Soak the cornhusks in warm water for at least 20 minutes, then rinse to remove any corn silk; drain well on paper towels.

Rehydrate the chiles in boiling water and remove seeds if you wish to reduce the heat level. Puree the chiles in a blender with enough of the boiling water to form a red chile sauce the consistency of runny ketchup. Combine the shredded meat and the chile sauce in a large saucepan and heat for 10 minutes.

Combine the corn flour, lard or shortening, baking powder, and salt in a large bowl. Add reserved broth a little at a time until it forms a thick, creamy, spreadable masa paste the consistency of soft peanut butter.

Spread ¼ cup of the masa mixture on the center of each cornhusk, then place 2 tablespoons of meat and sauce in the middle of the masa. Fold in the sides of the husks, then fold up the bottom, leaving the top open.

Place the tamales open side up inside a steamer insert of a large stockpot. Add water to the pot, cover, and steam the tamales for 40 minutes. To freeze leftover tamales, let them cool completely and then wrap them in a double layer of aluminum foil, making sure they are airtight before placing in the freezer.

Whiskey-Braised Lamb Shoulder

ALPENGLOW STUBE, KEYSTONE

Diners at the Stube enjoy breathtaking views as they ride the gondola to the top of the North Peak® at Keystone Resort. Sitting at 11,444 feet above sea level, the Stube is the highest AAA Four Diamond dining experience in North America, and its lamb shoulder is quite possibly the best meal served at any ski resort.

1 (3- to 5-pound) boneless lamb
   shoulder roast *(see Note)*

Salt and pepper

2 tablespoons canola oil

1 cup diced carrots

½ medium onion, diced

6 large garlic cloves, halved

2 teaspoons dried marjoram
   or oregano

¼ cup dried basil

¼ cup dried rosemary

1 bottle red wine

½ cup whiskey

1 to 4 cups hot lamb stock
   or chicken stock, as needed
   for braising

Makes 6 to 10 servings

Preheat the oven to 350 degrees. Trim the lamb shoulder of excess fat and season with salt and pepper. Heat a large Dutch oven over medium-high heat; add the oil and brown lamb on all sides.

Add the carrots, onions, and garlic and sweat the vegetables for a few minutes, then add the marjoram, basil, and rosemary. Deglaze the pan by adding the red wine and gently scraping the bottom of the pan; stir in the whiskey. Add enough hot lamb stock to come two-thirds of the way up the sides of the meat. Cover and place in the oven to cook until meat is very tender, about 2½ to 3 hours.

Transfer the lamb to a cutting board. Strain the braising liquid through a fine-mesh strainer into a large bowl and discard solids; reserve liquid to use as a sauce and season with salt and pepper to taste. Serve lamb with the sauce on creamy polenta (see recipe from Jennifer Jasinski on page 99), rice, or mashed potatoes.

❧ **Note:** *The lamb will cook down considerably over a long braise, so plan on about ¾ pound to 1 pound of pre-cooked lamb per serving.*

2 teaspoons fine sea salt

½ teaspoon lemon crystals,
    citric acid, or sour salt (optional)

1 tablespoon pepper

4 (6-ounce) buffalo or beef
    tenderloin steaks

Canola oil

1 tablespoon minced fresh
    flat-leaf parsley

2 to 3 tablespoons herb butter

Herb butter

1 medium shallot, chopped

1 clove garlic, minced

2 tablespoons chopped fresh
    flat-leaf parsley

2 tablespoons chopped
    fresh basil leaves

1 tablespoon snipped fresh chives

1 tablespoon chopped fresh
    cilantro leaves

1½ teaspoons fresh thyme leaves

1½ teaspoons chopped fresh
    rosemary leaves

2 cups (4 sticks) unsalted butter,
    at room temperature

1½ teaspoons fresh lemon juice

1 teaspoon kosher salt

1 to 2 tablespoons white wine

1 teaspoon Worcestershire sauce

Makes 4 servings

William Bent's Buffalo Tenderloin Filet Mignon

THE FORT™, MORRISON   ⚭   PROPRIETRESS HOLLY ARNOLD KINNEY

The smell of herb butter melting on a hot steak is intoxicating, and the leftover butter can be stored in the freezer for other uses. Take care not to overcook the meat because bison is lean and tends to be tough when cooked past medium rare.

Preheat the grill to high. Combine the sea salt, lemon crystals, and pepper. Season the steaks with the salt mixture, coating liberally on both sides, then brush lightly with oil.

Reduce grill heat to medium–high. Place the steaks about 6 inches from the heat and cook until the steaks are medium rare, about 10 to 18 minutes, depending on thickness, turning steaks every 4 minutes. Sprinkle with parsley and lay a disk of herb butter on top of each steak before serving.

For the herb butter:
Place the shallot, garlic, parsley, basil, chives, cilantro, thyme, and rosemary in a food processor. Pulse on and off until finely minced.

Put the butter in the bowl of an electric stand mixer fitted with the paddle attachment and add the herb mixture, lemon juice, salt, white wine, and Worcestershire sauce; beat until all the ingredients are fully incorporated and the mixture is smooth.

Wrap the herb butter in two pieces of plastic wrap, forming it into two logs, about 2 inches in diameter. Place in the refrigerator or freezer until firm before using. Herb butter may be stored in the refrigerator for several days and in the freezer for up to 2 months. Use herb butter on meats, vegetables, or bread.

Desserts & Sweet Treats

Raspberry-Marsala Cake, p. 149

4 cups whole milk

1 cup extra-fine sugar

1 tablespoon vanilla paste
   (see Sources on page 154)

½ cup cornstarch

10 large egg yolks

4 tablespoons unsalted butter

¾ cup (1½ sticks) salted butter

½ cup water

3 tablespoons dark corn syrup

1 pound brown sugar

2 tablespoons vanilla extract

2 tablespoons apple cider vinegar

6 bananas, sliced

¼ to ½ cup shaved chocolate,
   for garnish

12 tablespoons whipped cream,
   for topping

Makes 12 servings

Butterscotch and Banana Pudding

AJAX TAVERN AT THE LITTLE NELL, ASPEN   &   CHEF DANIELLE REISZ

The delicious blend of butterscotch, banana, and chocolate flavors makes this pudding irresistible. It's a staple on the menu at Ajax Tavern.

Warm the milk, extra-fine sugar, and vanilla paste in a medium saucepan, stirring until well combined. Combine the cornstarch and a small amount of the warm milk mixture in a small bowl to make a slurry. When the slurry is completely smooth, whisk in the egg yolks and set aside. Bring the remaining milk mixture to a boil and quickly whisk a small amount of the hot milk into the egg and cornstarch slurry. Pour the egg slurry back into the boiling milk mixture, whisking vigorously until the custard becomes thick and the cornstarch is cooked out, about 3 minutes. Pour the custard into a large bowl, whisk in the unsalted butter, and set aside.

Melt the salted butter in a large saucepan, and then stir in the water, corn syrup, and brown sugar. Bring to a boil and cook to 250 degrees on a candy thermometer. Pour the brown sugar mixture into the warm custard, whisking vigorously to make a smooth butterscotch pudding. Whisk in the vanilla extract and vinegar. Chill until set.

To assemble:
Layer sliced bananas on the bottom of twelve individual serving dishes and spoon pudding over top of the bananas. Sprinkle chocolate shavings over top of the pudding, add another layer of sliced bananas, and top with chocolate shavings again. Spoon more pudding over top of shavings, top with whipped cream, garnish with more chocolate shavings, and serve.

& ***Note:*** *If the pudding does not set up as firmly as you would like, you may gently reheat it, whisk in more cornstarch slurry until it thickens, cook for 3 minutes to cook out the cornstarch, and then re-chill.*

Cake

4 large eggs

1½ cups canola oil

2¼ cups sugar

1 tablespoon vanilla extract

1½ cups chopped walnuts

1 cup shredded carrots
(about 2 large carrots)

3 cups flour

1 teaspoon salt

1 teaspoon baking soda

¾ teaspoon baking powder

1 tablespoon cinnamon

Frosting

8 ounces cream cheese,
at room temperature

1 teaspoon vanilla extract

1 pound powdered sugar

Makes 10 to 12 servings

Carrot Cake

THE BRADLEY BOULDER INN, BOULDER & KATIE COBLE

Katie makes her carrot cake in a Bundt pan instead of a traditional cake pan, which makes for a pretty presentation of this moist cake. Either make the cream cheese frosting according to the instructions or thin the frosting to drizzle like a glaze.

For the cake:
Preheat the oven to 350 degrees. Lightly beat the eggs in a large mixing bowl using an electric mixer, and then add the oil, sugar, and vanilla and mix together. Mix in the walnuts and carrots. Add the flour, salt, baking soda, baking powder, and cinnamon; beat until combined, but do not over-mix.

Spray a 12-cup Bundt pan with cooking spray and pour the batter into the prepared pan. Set the pan on the center rack of the oven and bake until the edges of the cake have pulled away from the side of the pan and a toothpick inserted in the center comes out clean, about 45 to 55 minutes.

Cool the cake in the pan for 15 minutes, and then turn the cake out on a wire rack and let cool completely, at least 3 hours.

For the frosting:
Beat all ingredients together until creamy and spreadable. If desired, add small amounts of water to thin the frosting and use as a glaze. Frost or glaze the cake with the cream cheese frosting.

Cake

1 to 2 tablespoons ground red chili powder, mild or hot, to taste

2 cups water, divided

1 tablespoon vanilla extract

1 cup plus 2 tablespoons flour

1 cup plus 2 tablespoons cake flour (not self-rising, *see Guidelines for Recipes on page xviii*)

2 cups sugar

1 teaspoon baking soda

½ teaspoon salt

½ cup unsweetened, non-alkalized cocoa powder

1 cup (2 sticks) unsalted butter, cut into pieces and softened

½ cup buttermilk

2 large eggs, at room temperature

Chili-Chocolate Bourbon Cake

THE FORT™, MORRISON
PROPRIETRESS HOLLY ARNOLD KINNEY

The Fort™ serves a complimentary slice of this fudgy cake to any diner marking a special occasion, with staff in ceremonial headdress shouting the famous toast, "Hip, hip, huzzah!"

For the cake:

Preheat the oven to 350 degrees with a rack in the center. Butter two 9-inch round cake pans; lightly dust the sides of the pans with flour, tap out the excess, and line the bottom with circles of parchment paper.

Cook the chili powder in 1 cup of the water in a medium saucepan over medium heat until simmering. Remove the pan from the heat, stir in the vanilla, and set aside.

Using an electric stand mixer with a wire whip attachment for best results, combine the flour, cake flour, sugar, baking soda, salt, and cocoa and beat on low speed until well mixed. Add the softened butter to the dry mixture and beat thoroughly on medium-low speed. The mixture should have a uniform grainy texture.

Increase the speed to medium and gradually add the remaining 1 cup of water and the buttermilk. Add the eggs, one at a time, beating well after each addition. Slowly add the hot water-and-chili mixture to the batter and continue to beat just until well combined; be sure not to over-beat. Pour the mixture equally into the pans and bake until a toothpick inserted in the center of each layer comes out clean, about 35 to 40 minutes.

To cool, set the pans on a wire rack for 15 minutes, and then turn the cakes out onto the rack. Remove the parchment paper and immediately invert the cakes so that the risen tops don't flatten. Let the layers cool completely before frosting.

Frosting

¾ cup (1 ½ sticks) unsalted
    butter, softened

¾ cup unsweetened,
    non-alkalized cocoa powder

¼ cup plus 2 tablespoons
    buttermilk

4 to 5 cups powdered sugar

2 to 3 tablespoons bourbon

1 tablespoon vanilla extract

1 ½ cups chopped walnuts,
    lightly toasted (optional)

Makes 16 servings

For the frosting:

Combine the butter and cocoa in a large saucepan and melt over medium heat. Remove from the heat and stir in the buttermilk. Add the powdered sugar, a little at a time, stirring with a wire whisk between additions. Stir in the bourbon and vanilla and continue to whisk until the frosting is smooth and glossy. The frosting will stiffen as it cools, but in warm weather you may need to refrigerate it. Cool to a spreadable consistency.

To assemble:

If necessary, trim the tops of the cakes so that they are level. Place one of the cake layers on a 9-inch round cardboard cake circle. Spread 1 cup of the frosting over the layer. Sprinkle 1 cup of the chopped walnuts evenly over the frosting. Place the second layer of cake on the frosted base. Use the remaining frosting to cover the top and sides of the cake. Press the remaining walnuts into the frosting, covering the sides and top of the cake.

❦ **Note:** *Cocoa powders like Hershey's, Nestlé, or Ghiradelli are non-alkalized. Do not use Dutch process cocoa in this recipe. This cake is best when made 1 to 2 days before serving, as it gives the flavors time to blend.*

¼ cup dried cherries

¼ cup fresh cherries or pie
   cherries rinsed of any syrup

4 large eggs

9 ounces dark or semi-sweet
   chocolate

4 tablespoons butter

3 tablespoons sugar

½ cup plus 2 tablespoons
   heavy cream

Makes 8 servings

Chocolate-Cherry Mousse

SKI TIP LODGE, KEYSTONE & EXECUTIVE CHEF KEVIN MCCOMBS

Chocolate and cherries work wonderfully together, and this creamy mousse would be perfect for Valentine's Day.

Rehydrate the dried cherries in boiling water. Combine with the fresh cherries and then puree in the food processor until smooth.

Separate the eggs and retain both the yolks and whites. Combine the chocolate and butter in the top of a double boiler and melt. After the chocolate is melted, whisk in the cherry puree and egg yolks and return the pan to the double boiler to make sure chocolate doesn't cool too much.

Combine the egg whites and sugar in a small bowl and whip to medium peaks. Fold into the melted chocolate mixture in three stages. Whip cream to medium peaks and fold into chocolate mixture in three stages. Spoon the mousse into eight ramekins or other small serving dishes and refrigerate for at least 30 minutes before serving.

¾ cup brown sugar

¾ cup (1½ sticks) butter

2 large eggs

1 teaspoon vanilla extract

2½ cups flour

1 teaspoon baking soda

6 ounces semi-sweet
  chocolate chunks

5 ounces white chocolate chips

¼ cup chopped walnuts

Yields 2 dozen cookies

Chocolate Chunk-
White Chocolate Chip Cookies

HOLDEN HOUSE 1902 BED & BREAKFAST INN,
COLORADO SPRINGS   ❧   SALLIE CLARK

*The Holden House bottomless cookie jar is always a hit with bed
and breakfast guests, and these satisfying cookies are a favorite during
afternoon tea.*

Preheat the oven to 375 degrees. Combine the brown sugar and
butter in a large microwave-safe bowl and heat on high until soft,
about 30 to 40 seconds. Whisk in the eggs and vanilla and mix well.
Add the flour and baking soda and stir until well mixed. Stir in the
semi-sweet chocolate chunks, white chocolate chips, and walnuts.

Spoon well-rounded teaspoons of cookie dough onto an ungreased
insulated cookie sheet or traditional baking sheet and bake until
cookies are slightly brown on top, about 10 to 12 minutes.

1 sheet puff pastry dough, thawed but still chilled

½ cup sugar

¼ cup brown sugar

1 tablespoon cinnamon

4 golden delicious apples, peeled, cored, and thinly sliced

Makes 6 servings

Crisp Apple Tart

FLAGSTAFF HOUSE, BOULDER
EXECUTIVE CHEF AND PARTNER MARK MONETTE

This unusual presentation for an apple tart is really pretty and a nice way to serve individual tarts for a dinner party. Ready-to-use puff pastry dough can be found in the freezer section of the grocery store.

Preheat the oven to 350 degrees. Roll out the puff pastry until thin and cut six (4-inch) circles. Line a baking sheet with parchment paper or a silicone baking mat and place the puff pastry circles on the sheet. Combine the sugar, brown sugar, and cinnamon until well mixed. Toss the apple slices with half of the sugar mixture.

Sprinkle each circle of dough with about 1 tablespoon of the sugar mixture, and then assemble the apple slices on top of dough, over-lapping them as you circle the dough. Sprinkle the tops and around the sides with the remaining sugar mixture. Bake until golden brown, about 35 to 45 minutes.

Blueberry muffins

4 tablespoons unsalted butter, softened

Pinch salt

⅓ cup plus 1 tablespoon sugar

1 extra-large egg

¼ cup milk

1 cup flour

1 teaspoon baking powder

1 cup blueberries

Espresso Ice Cream Cakes with White Chocolate-Blueberry Crust

221 SOUTH OAK, TELLURIDE   ❧   CHEF/OWNER ELIZA H. S. GAVIN

Although created as simply a way to use up any leftover blueberry muffins from brunch at the restaurant, this dessert has since turned into one of chef Eliza Gavin's favorites.

For the blueberry muffins:

Preheat the oven to 325 degrees. Place the butter, salt, and ⅓ cup of sugar in the mixing bowl of an electric stand mixer fitted with the paddle attachment. Beat until the butter becomes slightly lighter in color, about 3 to 5 minutes. Scrape down the sides of the bowl. Add the egg while the mixer is on medium speed and, once the egg is combined, add half of the milk.

Sift together the flour and baking powder in a separate bowl. Add half of the flour mixture to the butter mixture, then the remaining milk, and then the remaining flour mixture. Add the blueberries to the mixing bowl and mix just until combined.

Spray a muffin tin with nonstick cooking spray and divide the batter between eight muffin cups. Sprinkle the remaining sugar over the muffins and bake for 10 to 15 minutes, or until a toothpick inserted into the center comes out clean. Cool slightly before turning muffins out of the muffin tin.

For the ice cream cakes:

Wrap wax paper or plastic wrap around the bottom of eight (3-inch) ring molds and secure with rubber bands. Heat water in the bottom of a double boiler to boiling and then reduce to simmer. Whisk together the egg yolks, sugar, water, and espresso powder in the top of the double boiler and continue whisking the yolk mixture constantly until the yolks are thick and warmed to 175 degrees on an instant-read thermometer, about 10 minutes. Set the yolk mixture aside to cool.

Ice cream cakes

11 large egg yolks

1 cup sugar

¼ cup water

2 tablespoons finely ground
    espresso powder

2 tablespoons Grand Marnier

2 tablespoons orange juice

1 teaspoon ground cinnamon

½ cup sour cream

1½ cups heavy cream

1 cup white chocolate chips

½ cup (1 stick) butter

8 blueberry muffins,
    recipe on previous page,
    or use store-bought

2 cups blueberries, plus more
    for garnish

Makes 8 servings

Combine the Grand Marnier, orange juice, cinnamon, sour cream, and whipping cream in the bowl of an electric stand mixer fitted with the whisk attachment and whisk on high until thick, about 5 minutes. Reduce the mixer speed to medium and slowly add the yolk mixture. Once the mixture is combined, divide the ice cream batter among the prepared molds. The batter should only fill the molds about two-thirds, leaving room to add the crust. Freeze the ice cream cakes until firm, about 8 hours.

After the ice cream cakes have frozen, prepare the crust. Place the white chocolate chips in a food processor. Melt the butter on high in the microwave until it is melted and hot, about 2 minutes. With the food processor running, add the hot butter to the white chocolate chips, melting the chocolate. Break up the muffins and add them and the blueberries to the food processor; puree the ingredients until smooth. Use a spatula to layer the crust mixture over the ice cream cakes in the ring molds. Freeze for 2 hours.

Presentation:
Unmold the cakes with the blueberry crust on the bottom and serve with additional blueberries as a garnish.

Cheesecake

10 tablespoons (1¼ sticks) butter, melted

6 ounces vanilla wafers (such as Nilla Wafers), finely ground (about 40 to 50 wafers)

2 ounces powdered sugar (about ½ cup)

½ teaspoon salt

¼ teaspoon cinnamon

8 ounces cream cheese, at room temperature

1½ pounds whole milk ricotta cheese

1 cup sugar

½ lemon, zested and juiced

1 teaspoon vanilla paste
   (see Sources on page 154)
   or 1 tablespoon vanilla extract

4 large eggs

Rhubarb compote

1 tablespoon butter

2 pounds rhubarb, diced

½ cup sugar

Pinch salt

¼ cup red wine

2 tablespoons red wine vinegar

1 tablespoon lemon juice

1 tablespoon cornstarch

Makes 10 to 12 servings

Fruition Farms Ricotta Cheesecake

FRUITION RESTAURANT, DENVER ❧ EXECUTIVE CHEF ALEX SIEDEL

The chef at Fruition serves this creamy cheesecake with rhubarb compote, but it's equally good topped with your fruit of choice.

For the cheesecake:
Combine the butter, wafers, powdered sugar, salt, and cinnamon in a bowl and stir with a spatula until well mixed. Butter the inside of a 9-inch springform pan; sprinkle the dough evenly over the bottom of the pan and press it down firmly; set aside.

Preheat the oven to 325 degrees. Place the cream cheese in the bowl of an electric stand mixer fitted with the paddle attachment and mix until soft and slightly whipped. Add the ricotta and mix on low until well combined. Add the sugar, lemon zest, lemon juice, and vanilla and mix on low until well combined. Add the eggs one at a time and mix until well incorporated. Scrape the paddle and bottom of the bowl with a spatula and mix to combine.

Pour the mixture over the prepared crust in the springform pan. Create a water bath by placing the springform pan in a large pan, and then fill the larger pan with water halfway up the side of the springform pan. Place into oven and bake until set, about 1½ to 2 hours. Serve with rhubarb compote, or fresh fruit of your choice.

For the rhubarb compote:
Add the butter and diced rhubarb to a large saucepan over medium heat and sweat the rhubarb until slightly softened. Add the sugar, salt, red wine, and vinegar and cook until the rhubarb is just starting to break down. Whisk the lemon juice and cornstarch together in a small bowl and quickly stir into the rhubarb to thicken. Cook just until the cornstarch slurry thickens and the rhubarb is cooked through. Pour into a bowl and refrigerate until chilled.

(see photograph on page x)

5 ounces dark chocolate

2 ounces unsweetened chocolate

½ cup (1 stick) butter

3 tablespoons cocoa powder

3 large eggs

1 ¼ cups sugar

½ teaspoon salt

2 teaspoons vanilla extract

1 cup flour

Yields 9 large or 16 small brownies

Fudge Brownies

VISTA VERDE GUEST RANCH, STEAMBOAT SPRINGS
CHEF MATT CAMPBELL

Vista Verde Guest Ranch tells its visitors that the cuisine balances between "ranchy and fancy," and these fudge brownies are sure to please everyone.

Preheat the oven to 350 degrees. Spray an 11 x 9 x 2-inch baking pan with baking spray, line the bottom of the pan with parchment paper, and then spray the parchment with baking spray.

Melt the dark chocolate, unsweetened chocolate, and butter in the top of a double boiler placed over simmering water; when melted, stir in the cocoa powder. Whisk together the eggs, sugar, salt, and vanilla in a large bowl. Whisk the melted chocolate into the egg mixture and then stir in the flour.

Pour the batter into the prepared pan and bake until slightly puffed and a toothpick inserted in the middle comes out with a small amount of crumb on it, about 35 to 45 minutes. Cool completely, about 2 hours, before cutting into squares.

Cupcakes

¾ cup unsweetened cocoa powder, plus more for dusting finished cupcakes

2 cups sugar

2 cups flour

1 teaspoon baking soda

Pinch salt

1 12-ounce bottle Left Hand Milk Stout beer

½ cup (1 stick) butter, melted

1 tablespoon vanilla extract

3 large eggs

8 ounces sour cream

Frosting

8 ounces cream cheese, at room temperature

1 pound powdered sugar

Yields 24 cupcakes

Milk Stout Cupcakes

LEFT HAND BREWING, LONGMONT

The folks at Left Hand say that milk sugar in your stout is like cream in your coffee. Nobody will ever guess that beer is the secret ingredient in these incredibly moist and creamy chocolate cupcakes.

For the cupcakes:
Preheat the oven to 350 degrees. Lightly grease 24 muffin cups or line with paper liners and spray with cooking spray. Combine the cocoa, sugar, flour, baking soda, and salt in a large bowl and whisk together.

Whisk together the stout, melted butter, and vanilla in a large bowl. Beat in the eggs one at time. Add the sour cream and mix until thoroughly combined and smooth. Gradually mix the flour mixture into the beer mixture.

Divide the batter equally among the muffin cups and bake, rotating the pans halfway through, until the cupcakes are raised, nicely domed, and set in the middle, about 20 to 25 minutes. Cool completely.

For the frosting:
Place the cream cheese in a large bowl and beat using an electric mixer on medium speed until light and fluffy. Reduce the speed to low and slowly mix in powdered sugar until incorporated and smooth. Top each cupcake with frosting and dust with cocoa.

⤙ **Note:** *Icing may be made several hours ahead and kept covered and chilled, but bring to room temperature before using to make it easier to spread. If you like a heavily frosted cupcake, double the icing recipe.*

Crust

1¼ cup (2½ sticks) butter,
    at room temperature

½ cup plus 2 tablespoons sugar

½ teaspoon salt

½ teaspoon vanilla extract

1 large egg

2¼ cups flour

Almond crème

½ cup (1 stick) butter,
    at room temperature

1¼ cups sugar

2 cups almond flour
    (also called almond meal)

2 large eggs

1 large egg yolk

1 tablespoon flour

Pears

5 pears

6 cups water

⅓ cup sugar

1 cinnamon stick

2 star anise

1 vanilla bean, split lengthwise

Makes 6 to 8 servings

Pear Tart

FLAGSTAFF HOUSE, BOULDER
EXECUTIVE CHEF AND PARTNER, MARK MONETTE

The Flagstaff House, built as a summer cabin by a Chicago schoolteacher in 1929, was converted to a summer restaurant in the 1950s. The Monette family expanded the property, converted it to a year-round restaurant in the early 1970s, and has operated the restaurant ever since.

For the crust:
Beat the butter and sugar together in a large bowl using an electric mixer, and then add the salt, vanilla, and egg and mix until well combined. Add the flour and mix just until dough comes together, taking care not to over-mix. Wrap the dough in plastic wrap and refrigerate before using.

For the almond crème:
Beat the butter and sugar together in a large bowl using an electric mixer, and then add the almond flour. Add the eggs and the yolk one at a time, stirring constantly; add the flour and mix until well combined.

For the pears:
Peel and quarter the pears, removing seeds and stems. Place the pears in a medium saucepan and cover with the water. Add the sugar, cinnamon stick, and star anise; scrape the seeds from the vanilla bean into the water. Bring to a simmer and cook for 10 to 15 minutes, and then drain and let cool.

To assemble:
Preheat the oven to 350 degrees. Roll out the chilled dough between two sheets of plastic wrap into a 13-inch circle. Remove the plastic wrap and press the dough into a nonstick 11-inch tart pan with a removable bottom. Place the pears in the shell and pour the almond crème over the pears; bake the tart for 45 minutes. Let cool slightly before removing tart from the pan and slicing.

(see photograph on page xx)

Crust

1 cup flour

¼ teaspoon salt

⅓ cup sugar

11 tablespoons (1 stick plus
   3 tablespoons) butter,
   cut into cubes, chilled

3 egg yolks

1 teaspoon vanilla extract

½ teaspoon red wine vinegar

Filling

3 cups chopped plums
   (about 1¼ pounds, *see Note*)

3 cups chopped nectarines
   (about 1¼ pounds, *see Note*)

½ cup sugar

1 tablespoon cornstarch

Juice of 1 small lemon
   (about 3 tablespoons)

Crumb topping

1½ cups flour

¾ cup brown sugar

⅓ cup sugar

¼ teaspoon salt

¼ teaspoon cinnamon

⅛ teaspoon ground sage

1 ounce bleu cheese, softened

¾ cup (1½ sticks) butter,
   melted and cooled

Makes 8 servings

Plum-Nectarine Crumble

LARKSPUR RESTAURANT, VAIL
CULINARY DIRECTOR THOMAS SALAMUNOVICH

*Although it may sound unusual, the addition of sage and bleu cheese
in the crumb topping of this dessert really makes the dish.*

For the crust:
Preheat the oven to 350 degrees. Place the flour, salt, sugar, and cold
butter in the bowl of an electric stand mixer and mix on low until
butter is the size of peas. Add the egg yolks, vanilla, and vinegar and
mix just until dough starts to come together. Remove bowl from
mixer and continue mixing by hand until uniform, taking care not to
handle the dough too much or the butter will begin to melt. Shape
the dough into a disk, wrap in plastic, and refrigerate for 30 minutes.

Roll out the dough between two pieces of wax paper to ⅛-inch
thickness. Spray a 9-inch pie pan with cooking spray and press crust
into the pan; trim the excess dough from the rim. Line the crust with
parchment paper, fill with dried beans, and bake for 15 minutes.
Remove the beans and paper and continue baking until the crust
is light brown in color and dry, about 10 more minutes; set aside.

For the filling:
Toss the plums and nectarines with the sugar, cornstarch, and lemon
juice. Add filling to the pre-baked pie crust.

For the crumb topping:
Place the flour, brown sugar, sugar, salt, cinnamon, and sage in a
large bowl and mix until fully incorporated. Crumble in the bleu
cheese and use your fingers to mix it into the dry ingredients.
Pour in the melted butter and stir until mixture is crumbly.

Spoon the crumb mixture generously over the filling and bake until
the fruit filling oozes and bubbles over the edges and the crumb
topping is golden brown, about 20 minutes.

☙ ***Note:*** *The Larkspur peels their plums and nectarines before preparing this
   dessert, but this step is optional.*

(see photograph on page xi)

½ cup dry Marsala

¼ cup freshly squeezed
    orange juice

1 ½ cups flour

1 teaspoon baking powder

1 teaspoon salt

¼ teaspoon baking soda

¼ teaspoon nutmeg

14 tablespoons butter (1 ¾ sticks),
    at room temperature, divided

1 ¼ cups sugar, divided

2 large eggs

1 teaspoon vanilla extract

1 teaspoon lemon zest

4 cups fresh raspberries, divided

2 tablespoons vanilla sugar
    (or powdered sugar)

2 cups crème fraîche

Makes 8 servings

Raspberry-Marsala Cake

VISTA VERDE GUEST RANCH, STEAMBOAT SPRINGS
EXECUTIVE CHEF MATT CAMPBELL

*Vista Verde uses wild raspberries to top this simple, sweet cake. Don't be
concerned about the rustic appearance of the cake when it's removed from
the oven, as it will be topped with crème fraîche and fresh raspberries.*

Preheat the oven to 400 degrees. Grease a 10-inch springform pan
and line the bottom with parchment paper. Combine the Marsala
and orange juice and set aside. Sift together the flour, baking powder,
salt, baking soda, and nutmeg and set aside.

Combine ¾ cup (1½ sticks) of the butter and 1 cup of the sugar in the
bowl of an electric stand mixer and beat until well mixed. With the
mixer running, slowly add the eggs, vanilla extract, and lemon zest,
making sure to incorporate fully. Add a bit of the Marsala mixture
and then a bit of the flour mixture, and continue adding alternately
until both are well combined.

Spoon the batter into the prepared pan and sprinkle with 1½ cups of
the raspberries. Bake until the top is just barely set, about 20 minutes.

Remove the cake from the oven and reduce the oven temperature to
375 degrees. Dot the cake with the remaining 2 tablespoons of butter
and sprinkle with the remaining sugar. Bake until a toothpick inserted
in the middle of the cake comes out clean, about 10 minutes longer.

Remove the cake and allow to cool for a few minutes. Run a knife
around the outer rim of the springform pan and then let the cake
cool fully, about 30 minutes, before removing from the pan.

To serve, combine the vanilla sugar with crème fraîche and spoon
over the top of cake slices. Garnish with remaining raspberries.

(see photograph on page 133)

4 tablespoons butter

4 Colorado peaches, skinned,
   pitted, and cut in half

3 sprigs fresh thyme

2 vanilla beans, cut lengthwise
   to expose seeds

4 ounces honey (about ⅓ cup)

1 (375-ml) bottle of
   Baume de Venise dessert wine
   (see Sources on page 154)

3 tablespoons pistachio paste,
   or more to taste
   (see Sources on page 154)

¾ cup sugar

4 large eggs

1¾ cups milk

½ cup heavy cream

1 loaf brioche bread,
   crusts trimmed, cut into
   4-inch x 1-inch logs

1 tablespoon butter, for cooking
   brioche bread pudding

Powdered sugar, for dusting
   (optional)

4 cups high-quality vanilla bean
   ice cream

Makes 8 servings

Roasted Colorado Peach-Pistachio Brioche Pudding with Ice Cream

THE BROADMOOR, COLORADO SPRINGS
EXECUTIVE PASTRY CHEF REMY FÜNFROCK

At the Broadmoor, Chef Remy Fünfrock makes brioche with pistachios to enhance the pistachio flavor and serves the dessert with an unusual Muscovado sugar ice cream. To reduce the complexity in the recipe for home cooks, I've substituted store-bought brioche and vanilla bean ice cream.

Preheat the oven to 375 degrees. Heat the butter in an oven–safe sauté pan over high heat until light brown in color. Place peach halves flat side down in the hot butter and add the thyme and vanilla beans. Cook, shaking the pan from time to time to prevent peaches from sticking, until peaches take on a golden brown color.

Reduce heat to medium and add the honey to the pan. Flip the peaches over and pour in the Baume de Venise. Place the pan in the oven and finish cooking the peaches until tender, 10 to 15 minutes. When done, remove from the oven and reserve the juices.

While the peaches are cooking, prepare the brioche pudding. Mix together the pistachio paste, sugar, and eggs in a medium bowl, and then stir in the milk and heavy cream until well mixed. Dip the brioche logs in the pistachio batter. Heat a skillet over medium–high heat and melt the butter; cook the brioche on both sides as you would French toast.

Presentation:

To serve, place a warm peach half on each of eight plates. Place pistachio brioche pieces overlapping the peach and dust with powdered sugar. Serve with a scoop of high-quality vanilla bean ice cream and drizzle the plate with juices from the roasted peach. Serve immediately.

Originally a ranch growing corn to make brooms, later a dairy farm, and then a casino, The Broadmoor was eventually purchased in 1916 by Spencer Penrose, a Philadelphia entrepreneur who had made his fortune in gold and copper mining. Penrose was intent on building the most beautiful resort in the world, and today, sitting on 3,000 acres under the shadow of Cheyenne Mountain outside Colorado Springs, The Broadmoor is the longest-running consecutive winner of both the AAA Five Diamond and Forbes Travel Guide Five Star awards.

Butter and sugar, for preparing
   ramekins

4 ounces Valrhona Caraibe
   chocolate or other high-quality
   dark chocolate (65% cacao)

½ cup (1 stick) unsalted butter

½ cup sugar

5 tablespoons cornstarch

2 large eggs

2 large egg yolks

¼ cup crushed, toasted
   macadamia nuts

Powdered sugar, for dusting

Crème Anglaise sauce
   (optional; see Note)

Mint leaves, for garnish (optional)

Makes 6 servings

Valrhona Chocolate-Macadamia Nut Cake with Vanilla-Bourbon Anglaise

SONNENALP RESORT, VAIL   ∾   EXECUTIVE CHEF STEFAN SCHMID

These dense flourless chocolate cakes are rich and fudgy and can be prepared a day in advance for a dinner party.

Preheat the oven to 250 degrees. Butter six ramekins thoroughly, then shake on sugar to evenly coat. Melt the chocolate and butter together over a double boiler; mix thoroughly and cool. Combine the sugar and cornstarch and stir into melted chocolate mixture. Slowly whisk in the eggs and yolks; do not over–mix. Sprinkle the macadamia nuts into bottom of ramekins and divide the batter equally among the ramekins.

Bake until the cakes are lightly set and have risen slightly, about 20 to 35 minutes. Judge doneness by looking through the oven window; do not open the oven during baking or the cakes could fall.

Invert the cakes onto flat plates and dust with powdered sugar to taste. If desired, serve with crème Anglaise sauce. Garnish with mint leaves.

∾ **Note:** *To prepare crème Anglaise sauce, heat ½ cup milk in a small saucepan over medium heat just until scalding. Whisk together 2 egg yolks and 2 tablespoons of sugar, and then quickly whisk into the hot milk. Continue cooking over medium heat, stirring constantly, until the sauce has thickened. Stir in 1 tablespoon bourbon, if desired, and serve immediately.*

1/4 cup water

1 envelope unflavored gelatin

1 1/4 cups heavy cream

1/2 cup sugar

2 cups plain yogurt
    (Greek yogurt is best)

1 teaspoon vanilla extract

Makes 6 servings

Yogurt Panna Cotta

SILVER QUEEN BED & BREAKFAST, GEORGETOWN
OWNER JOYCE JAMELE

At the inn, Joyce serves her silky panna cotta dessert with sliced strawberries sprinkled with sugar or with a simple blueberry sauce made by simmering blueberries with a bit of sugar and water.

Pour the water into a small bowl, sprinkle gelatin over it, and let stand for 10 minutes. Bring the cream and sugar to a simmer in a medium saucepan over medium heat, stirring until sugar dissolves.

Remove from the heat and whisk in the gelatin mixture until dissolved. Whisk in the yogurt and vanilla. Pour into six (6-ounce) ramekins and place them on a baking sheet. Cover with plastic wrap and refrigerate overnight.

Presentation:
Run a knife around the inside edge of each ramekin, and then place each ramekin in a shallow bowl of hot water for 10 seconds. Invert panna cotta onto a serving plate and top with fruit of your choice.

sources for specialty ingredients and other products

Alamosa striped bass: seattlefishnm.com

Alpine Avocado Vinaigrette: alpineavocado.com

Alta cucina tomatoes: stanislaus.com

Anson Mills white grits: ansonmills.com

Baume de Venise wine: in the French dessert wine section of fine wine shops

Colorado bison: bisoncentral.com/bison-buyers-guide

Colorado lamb: foxfirefarms.com

Demi-glace: available in fine food stores or through amazon.com

"First Snow" blue vein goat cheese: Jumpin' Good Goat Dairy, jumpingoodgoats.com

Fruition Farms ricotta cheese: The Truffle Cheese Shop in Denver, denvertruffle.com

Haystack Mountain goat cheese: haystackgoatcheese.com

Lamb stock: morethangourmet.com

Left Hand Milk Stout Beer: lefthandbrewing.com (use the Beer Finder)

Nueske's smoked chicken: nueskes.com

Pistachio paste: kingarthurflour.com/shop/items/all-natural-pistachio-paste-11-oz

Rabbit: available in specialty butcher shops or through dartagnan.com

Vanilla paste: beanilla.com or williams-sonoma.com

contributors

221 South Oak
221 South Oak Street
Telluride, CO 81435
(970) 728-9507
221southoak.com

Alpenglow Stube
Keystone Mountain
Keystone, CO 80435
(800) 354-4386
keystoneresort.com

Barolo Grill
3030 East Sixth Avenue
Denver, CO 80206
(303) 393-1040
barologrilldenver.com

Beaumont Hotel & Spa
Bulow's Bistro
505 Main Street
PO Box 1265
Ouray, CO 81427
(970) 325-7000
beaumonthotel.com

Bittersweet
500 East Alameda Avenue
Denver, CO 80209
(303) 942-0320
bittersweetdenver.com

Blackbelly Catering
PO Box 7461
Boulder, CO 80306
(720) 427-8386
blackbellycatering.com

The Bradley Boulder Inn
2040 Sixteenth Street
Boulder, CO 80302
(303) 545-5200
thebradleyboulder.com

Briar Rose Bed & Breakfast
2151 Arapahoe Avenue
Boulder, CO 80302
briarrosebb.com
(303) 442-3007

The Broadmoor
The Penrose Room
1 Lake Avenue
Colorado Springs, CO 80907
(719) 577-5733
broadmoor.com

The Buckhorn Exchange
1000 Osage Street
Denver, CO 80204
(303) 534-9505
buckhorn.com

C Lazy U Ranch
3640 Colorado Highway 125
Granby, CO 80446
(970) 887-3344
clazyu.com

Café Diva
1855 Ski Time Square Drive
Steamboat Springs, CO 80487
(970) 871-0508
cafediva.com

Capitol Hill Mansion
1207 Pennsylvania Street
Denver, CO 80203
(303) 839-5221
capitolhillmansion.com

Caribou Club
411 East Hopkins Avenue
Aspen, CO 81611
(970) 925-2929
caribouclub.com

Castle Marne Bed and Breakfast
1572 Race Street
Denver, CO 80206
(303) 331-0621
castlemarne.com

ChoLon Modern Asian Bistro
1555 Blake Street, #101
Denver, CO 80202
(303) 353-5223
cholon.com

The Cliff House
306 Canon Avenue
Manitou Springs, CO 80829
(719) 785-1000
thecliffhouse.com

Colterra
210 Franklin Street
Niwot, CO 80544
(303) 652-0777
colterra.com

Cooking with Michele
2403 South Milwaukee Street
Denver, CO 80210
(720) 344-8173
cookingwithmichele.com

Devil's Thumb Ranch
3530 County Highway 83
Tabernash, CO 80478
(970) 726-5632
devilsthumbranch.com

Dunton Hot Springs
52068 West Fork Road, #38
Dolores, CO 81323
(970) 882-4800
duntonhotsprings.com

East Side Bistro
435 Sixth Street
Crested Butte, CO 81224
(970) 349-9699
eastsidebistro.com

Eastholme in the Rockies B&B
4445 Hagerman Avenue
Cascade, CO 80809
(719) 684-9901
eastholme.com

Flagstaff House
1138 Flagstaff Road
Boulder, CO 80302-9510
(303) 442-4640
flagstaffhouse.com

The Fort™, LLC
PO Box 569
19192 Highway 8
Morrison, CO 80465
(303) 697-4771
thefort.com

Frasca Food and Wine
1738 Pearl Street
Boulder, CO 80302
(303) 442-6966
frascafoodandwine.com

Fruition Restaurant
1313 East Sixth Avenue
Denver, CO 80218
(303) 831-1962
fruitionrestaurant.com

Hearthstone Restaurant
130 South Ridge Street
Breckenridge, CO 80424
(970) 453-1148
stormrestaurants.com

Highland Haven Creekside Inn
4395 Independence Trail
Evergreen, CO 80439
(303) 674-3577
highlandhaven.com

Holden House 1902
Bed & Breakfast Inn
1102 West Pikes Peak Avenue
Colorado Springs, CO 80904
(719) 471-3980
holdenhouse.com

Hooper Homestead
210 Hooper Street
Central City, CO 80427
(303) 582-5828
hooperhomestead.com

Hotel Boulderado
2115 Thirteenth Street
Boulder, CO 80302
(303) 442-4344
boulderado.com

Hotel Gasthof Gramshammer
Pepi's Restaurant
231 East Gore Creek Drive
Vail, CO 81657
(970) 476-5626
pepis.com

Hotel Jerome
Garden Terrace
330 East Main Street
Aspen, CO 81611
(970) 920-1000
hoteljerome.aubergeresorts.com

Hotel Monaco
Panzano
909 Seventeenth Street
Denver, CO 80202
(303) 296-3525
panzano-denver.com

Hotel Teatro
Restaurant Kevin Taylor
1106 Fourteenth Street
Denver, CO 80202
(303) 820-2600
ktrg.net

The Inn at Lost Creek
9545 Restaurant
119 Lost Creek Lane
Telluride, CO 81435-9503
(970) 728-5678
innatlostcreek.com

Jennifer Jasinski
Rioja, Bistro Vendome,
and Euclid Hall
1431 Larimer Street
Denver, CO 80202
(303) 802-2282
jenniferjasinski.com

Jenny Morris
savourthesensesblog.com

Kelly Liken
12 Vail Road, #100
Vail, CO 81657
(970) 479-0175
kellyliken.com

La Tour
122 East Meadow Drive
Vail, CO 81657
(970) 476-4403
latour-vail.com

Larkspur Restaurant
458 Vail Valley Drive
Vail, CO 81657
(970) 754-8050
larkspurvail.com

Left Hand Brewing
1265 Boston Avenue
Longmont, CO 80501
(303) 772-0258
lefthandbrewing.com

The Little Nell
Ajax Tavern
685 East Durant Avenue
Aspen, CO 81611
(970) 920-6334
thelittlenell.com/restaurants/ajax_tavern.aspx

The Little Nell
Montagna
675 East Durant Avenue
Aspen, CO 81611
(970) 920-6330
thelittlenell.com/restaurants/montagna-restaurant.aspx

Los Altos Bed & Breakfast
375 Hill View Drive
Grand Junction, CO 81507
(888) 774-0982
losaltosgrandjunction.com

Luca d'Italia
711 Grant Street
Denver, CO 80203
(303) 832-6600
lucadenver.com

Mariposa Lodge
855 Grand Street
Steamboat Springs, CO 80477
(970) 879-1467
steamboatmariposa.com

Mezcal
3230 East Colfax Avenue
Denver, CO 80206
(303) 322-5219
mezcalcolorado.com

Mizuna
225 East Seventh Avenue
Denver, CO 80203
(303) 832-4778
mizunadenver.com

New Belgium Brewery
500 Linden Street
Fort Collins, CO 80524
(970) 221-0524
newbelgium.com

North Fork Ranch
Box B
55395 Highway 285
Shawnee, CO 80475
(303) 838-9873
northforkranch.com

Old Town GuestHouse
115 South Twenty-sixth Street
Colorado Springs, CO 80904
(719) 632-9194
oldtown-guesthouse.com

Opus
2575 West Main Street
Littleton, CO 80120
(303) 703-6787
opusdine.com

Park Hyatt Beaver Creek
Resort and Spa
8100 Mountainside Bar & Grill
50 West Thomas Place
Avon, CO 81620
(970) 949-1234
hyatt.com/gallery/beave8100

The Pullman
330 Seventh Street
Glenwood Springs, CO 81601
(970) 230-9234
thepullmangws.com

The Ritz–Carlton, Bachelor Gulch
0130 Daybreak Ridge
Avon, CO 81620
(970) 748-6200
ritzcarlton.com/BachelorGulch

Romantic RiverSong Inn
1765 Lower Broadview Road
Estes Park, CO 80517
(970) 586-4666
romanticriversong.com

Root Down
1600 West Thirty-third Avenue
Denver, CO 80211
(303) 993-4200
rootdowndenver.com

The Ruby of Crested Butte
624 Gothic Avenue
Crested Butte, CO 81224
(800) 390-1338
therubyofcrestedbutte.com

Rustico
114 East Colorado Avenue
Telluride, CO 81435
(970) 728-4046
rusticoristorante.com

SALT the Bistro
1047 Pearl Street
Boulder, CO 80302
(303) 444-7258
saltboulderbistro.com

Silver Queen Bed & Breakfast
314 Argentine Street
Georgetown, CO 80444
(303) 569-3511
silverqueenbandb.com

Six89
689 Main Street
Carbondale, CO 81623
(970) 963-6890
six89.com

Ski Tip Lodge
764 Montezuma Road
Keystone, CO 80435
(800) 354-4386
keystoneresort.com

Sonnenalp Resort of Vail
20 Vail Road
Vail, CO 81657
(970) 476-5656
sonnenalp.com

St. Regis Aspen Resort
315 East Dean Street
Aspen, CO 81611
(970) 429-9562
stregisaspen.com

The Stanley Hotel
333 East Wonder View Avenue
Estes Park, CO 80517
(970) 577-4000
stanleyhotel.com

The Steamboat Grand
The Cabin
2300 Mount Werner Circle
Steamboat Springs, CO 80487
(800) 224-1431
steamboatgrand.com

The Strater Hotel
Mahogany Grille
699 Main Avenue
Durango, CO 81301
(970) 247-4433
mahoganygrille.com

Tables on Kearney
2267 Kearney Street
Denver, CO 80207-3921
(303) 388-0299
tablesonkearney.com

Tamayo
1400 Larimer Street
Denver, CO 80202-1744
(720) 946-1433
richardsandoval.com/tamayo

Vesta Dipping Grill
1822 Blake Street
Denver, CO 80202
(303) 296-1970
vestagrill.com

Viceroy Hotel
Eight K
PO Box 6985
130 Wood Road
Snowmass Village, CO 81615
(970) 923-8029
viceroyhotelsandresorts.com/snowmass

The Village Smithy
26 South Third Street
Carbondale, CO 81623
(970) 963-9990
villagesmithy.com

Vista Verde Guest Ranch
PO Box 770465
58000 Cowboy Way
Clark, CO 80428
(970) 879-3858
vistaverde.com

index

A

Ajax Baked Chèvre, 24
Alamosa Striped Bass, 92
almond crème, 147
almonds
    Heirloom Tomato Salad, 56–57
altitude, adjusting for, xviii
Amish Breakfast Casserole, *2,* 3
apples
    Braised Pork with Apples and Dijon, 93
    Crisp Apple Tart, 141
    Dutch Apple Pancake, 9
    Celeriac, Apple, and Fennel Salad, 40
Artichoke Bisque, *76,* 77
artichoke hearts
    Artichoke Bisque, *76,* 77
    Roast Colorado Lamb Chops, 120
    Artichoke, Tomato, and Olive Tapenade, 121
    Stewed Artichoke, 122–123
arugula
    Rocket Salad, *54,* 55
    Heirloom Tomato Salad, 56–57
    Warm Goat Cheese Salad, 73
asparagus
    Alamosa Striped Bass, 92
    Crisp Gnocchi Salad, 48
    Fondue, 104
    Lemon and Asparagus Risotto, 58
avocados
    Guacamole, 34

B

Baby Spinach and Bibb Lettuce Salad with Chipotle-Buttermilk
    Dressing, 46
bacon
    Amish Breakfast Casserole, *2,* 3
    Colorado Game Meatloaf, 98
    Wild Boar Bacon Vinaigrette, 39
    Wedge Salad, 74
bananas
    Butterscotch and Banana Pudding, 134
barley
    Farro and Barley "Risotto," *45,* 50
bass, striped
    Alamosa Striped Bass, 92
    Pan-Roasted Colorado Striped Bass, 114
beans
    Bison Chili, 78
    Fort's™ Famous Black Beans, The, 51
    Quinoa, Black Bean, and Corn Pilaf, 63
    Roast Colorado Lamb Chops with White Beans, 120
Bear Creek Smoked Trout Pâté, 25
beef
    Espresso-Rubbed Beef Tenderloin, 103
    New York Strip Steaks with Gonzales Sauce, 113
    William Bent's Buffalo Tenderloin Filet Mignon, 132

beef, ground
    Bison Chili, 78
    Colorado Game Meatloaf, 98
    Tagliatelle Pasta with White Bolognese, 129
beef stock
    Bison Chili, 78
    Lamb Jus, 99
    Green Chile Posole, 83
    Sautéed Brussels Sprouts with Chestnuts, 65
beer
    Milk Stout Cupcakes, 146
beets
    Warm Goat Cheese Salad with Pistachios
      and Baby Beets, 73
beurre blanc, 117–118
biscuits
    Goat Cheese Rosemary Biscuits, *32,* 33
bison
    Buffalo Redeye Stew, 79
    Braised Buffalo, 35–36
    William Bent's Buffalo Tenderloin Filet Mignon, 132
bison, ground
    Bison Chili, 78
Bison Chili, 78
blackberries
    Elk Chops with Blackberry Sauce, 101–102
blueberries
    Blueberry Cake Muffins, 4
    Blueberry French Toast Strata, 5
    White Chocolate-Blueberry Crust, 142–143
Blueberry Cake Muffins, 4
Blueberry French Toast Strata, 5
bourbon
    Buffalo Redeye Stew, 79
    Chili-Chocolate Bourbon Cake, 136–137
Braised Pork with Apples and Dijon, 93
bread
    Blueberry French Toast Strata, 5
    Chipotle-Steeped Mussels, *23,* 30
    Colorado Game Meatloaf, 98
    Crème Brûlée French Toast, 8
    Eggplant Croutons, 56
    Fondue, 104
    Lamb Slider, 109
    Olathe Sweet Corn Spoon Bread, 60
    Portobello and Sage Bread Pudding, 62
    Portobello Mushroom Burger, *91,* 116
    Roasted Colorado Peach-Pistachio Brioche Pudding, 150–151
    Southwestern Crab Cakes, *124,* 126
    Southwest Green Chile Toast, 21
    Spaghetti Squash Fritters, *66,* 67
bread pudding
    Portobello and Sage Bread Pudding, 62
Broiled Pancetta-Wrapped Dates Stuffed with Gorgonzola, 26
brownies
    Fudge Brownies, 145

Brussels sprouts
Sautéed Brussels Sprouts with Chestnuts, 65
Buffalo Redeye Stew, 79
burgers
Lamb Slider with Mint and Tomato-Ginger Chutney, 109
Portobello Mushroom Burger, 91, 116
buttermilk
Chipotle-Buttermilk Dressing, 46
butters, 28–29, 117–118, 152
Butterscotch and Banana Pudding, 134

C

cakes
Carrot Cake, 135
Chili-Chocolate Bourbon Cake, 136–137
Raspberry-Marsala Cake, *133*, 149
Valrhona Chocolate-Macadamia Nut Cake
with Vanilla-Bourbon Anglaise, 152
cantaloupe
Melon Ambrosia, 14
Carrot Cake, 135
carrots
Carrot Cake, 135
Fondue, 104
casseroles
Amish Breakfast Casserole, *2*, 3
Blueberry French Toast Strata, 5
Ham and Portobello Mushroom Casserole, 12
Sausage and Egg Casserole, 20
cauliflower
Cauliflower and Summer Vegetables, 47
Fondue, 104
Gingery Cauliflower Soup, 82
Cauliflower and Summer Vegetables, 47
celeriac
Celeriac, Apple, and Fennel Salad, 39–40
ceviche
Mahi-Mahi Ceviche, 37
chard
Swiss Chard and Gruyère Quiche, 22
cheese
Ajax Baked Chèvre, 24
Amish Breakfast Casserole, *2*, 3
Artichoke Bisque, *76*, 77
Broiled Pancetta-Wrapped Dates Stuffed with Gorgonzola, 26
Creamy Polenta, 100
Fondue, 104
Fruition Farms Ricotta Cheesecake, *x*, 144
Goat Cheese Rosemary Biscuits, *32*, 33
Ham and Portobello Mushroom Casserole, 12
Heirloom Tomato Salad with Fruition Farms Ricotta, 56–57
Lobster Mac and Cheese, 110, *111*
Mountain High Mac and Cheese, 112
Gorgonzola Sauce, 38
Portobello and Sage Bread Pudding, 62
Sausage and Egg Casserole, 20
Southwest Green Chile Toast, 21
Spaghetti Squash Fritters, *66*, 67
Stone-Ground Bleu Cheese Grits, 68
Summer Caprese Salad, *69*, 70
Swiss Chard and Gruyère Quiche, 22

Warm Goat Cheese Salad, 73
Wedge Salad with Saison-Ranch Dressing, 74
cheesecakes
Fruition Farms Ricotta Cheesecake, *x*, 144
cherries
Chocolate-Cherry Mousse, 138, *139*
chestnuts
Sautéed Brussels Sprouts with Chestnuts, 65
chicken
Chicken Stuffed with Mushrooms, Leeks, and Pistachios, 94
Garlic and Sage-Stuffed Chicken Breasts, 105
Jaeger Schnitzel with Wild Mushroom Sauce, 108
Mountain High Mac and Cheese, 112
North Fork Rabbit Hash with Poached Eggs, 15
Santa Fe Chicken Salad, 64
Slow-Poached Chicken, 122–123
Smoked Pheasant Soup, 87
chicken stock
Bison Chili, 78
Braised Pork with Apples and Dijon, 93
Creamy Polenta, 100
Cream of Cilantro Soup, 80
Gingery Cauliflower Soup, 82
Lemon and Asparagus Risotto, 58
Lentil Soup with Prosciutto Chips, 86
Mountain High Mac and Cheese, 112
Mushroom and Brown Butter Risotto, 59
New York Strip Steaks with Gonzales Sauce, 113
Stracciatella, 88
Whiskey-Braised Lamb Shoulder, 131
Chicken Stuffed with Mushrooms, Leeks, and Pistachios, 94
chickpeas
Sweet Potato Falafel with Lemon-Tahini Yogurt, 43
Chile-Citrus Shrimp with Coconut Rice and Red Curry
Vinaigrette, 95–96
Chile Crab Rolls with Charred Corn and Sriracha Mayo, 27
Chile Relleno of Crab, 28–29
chiles
Chile-Citrus Shrimp, 95–96
Chile Relleno of Crab, 28–29
Cowboy Corn Cakes, *6*, 7
Green Chile Posole, 83
Green Gazpacho, 84, *85*
Grilled Shrimp, 106–107
New York Strip Steaks with Gonzales Sauce, 113
Poblano Chile and Chive Mashed Potatoes, 61
Quinoa, Black Bean, and Corn Pilaf, 63
roasting, xx
Southwest Green Chile Toast, 21
taste-testing, xix
Traditional Home-Style Red Chile Pork Tamales, 130
See also chipotle; peppers, bell
Chile-Seasoned Pot-Roasted Pork, 97
chili
Bison Chili, 78
Green Chile Posole, 83
Chili-Chocolate Bourbon Cake, 136–137
chili powder, xix
chipotle
Chipotle-Buttermilk Dressing, 46
Chile-Seasoned Pot-Roasted Pork, 97

Chipotle-Steeped Mussels, *23*, 30
    puree, xix
    Raspberry-Chipotle Pork Tenderloin, 119
    See also chiles; peppers, bell
Chipotle-Steeped Mussels, *23*, 30
chocolate
    Chili-Chocolate Bourbon Cake, 136-137
    Chocolate-Cherry Mousse, 138, *139*
    Chocolate Chunk-White Chocolate Chip Cookies, 140
    White Chocolate-Blueberry Crust, 142-143
    Fudge Brownies, 145
    Milk Stout Cupcakes, 146
    Valrhona Chocolate-Macadamia Nut Cake, 152
Chocolate-Cherry Mousse, 138, *139*
Chocolate Chunk-White Chocolate Chip Cookies, 140
chorizo
    Alamosa Striped Bass, 92
    Crispy Chorizo-Corn Relish, 106-107
chutney, 109
cilantro
    Cream of Cilantro Soup, 80
    Green Chile Posole, 83
    Sweet Corn Soup with Cilantro Puree, 89
citrus juice
    Tequila-Orange Sauce, 106-107
    Blood Orange Beurre Blanc, 117-118
    Red Pepper-Citrus Sauce, 122-123
coconut
    Coconut Rice, 95-96
Colorado Game Meatloaf, 98
Colorado Leg of Lamb with Creamy Polenta and Lamb Jus, 99-100
cookies
    Chocolate Chunk-White Chocolate Chip Cookies, 140
corn
    Cauliflower and Summer Vegetables, 47
    Chile Crab Rolls with Charred Corn, 27
    Chile Relleno of Crab, 28-29
    Cowboy Corn Cakes, *6*, *7*
    Crispy Chorizo-Corn Relish, 106-107
    Olathe Sweet Corn Spoon Bread, 60
    Quinoa, Black Bean, and Corn Pilaf, 63
    Smoked Pheasant Soup, 87
    Sweet Corn Soup with Cilantro Puree, 89
corn flour
    Traditional Home-Style Red Chile Pork Tamales, 130
cottage cheese
    Bear Creek Smoked Trout Pâté, 25
Cowboy Corn Cakes, *6*, *7*
crab
    Artichoke Bisque, *76*, *77*
    Chile Crab Rolls, 27
    Chile Relleno of Crab, 28-29
    Southwestern Crab Cakes, *124*, 125-126
cranberries
    Orange, Cranberry, and Walnut Scones, *1*, 18
cream, xix
cream cheese
    Bear Creek Smoked Trout Pâté, 25
    Blueberry French Toast Strata, 5
    Carrot Cake, 135
    Fruition Farms Ricotta Cheesecake, *x*, 144

Cream of Cilantro Soup, 80
Crème Brûlée French Toast, 8
Crisp Apple Tart, 141
Crisp Gnocchi Salad with Wild Mushrooms
    and Asparagus, 48
crumbles
    Plum-Nectarine Crumble, *xi*, 148
crumb toppings, 148
cucumbers
    Green Gazpacho, 84, *85*
cupcakes
    Milk Stout Cupcakes, 146
Curried Butternut Squash Soup, *75*, 81

D
dates
    Broiled Pancetta-Wrapped Dates, 26
duck stock
    Braised Pork with Apples and Dijon, 93
Dutch Apple Pancake, *9*

E
eggnog
    Eggnog Muffins, 10
Eggnog Muffins, 10
eggplant
    Eggplant Caponata, 49
    Eggplant Croutons, 56-57
Eggplant Caponata, 49
eggs
    Amish Breakfast Casserole, *2*, 3
    Blueberry French Toast Strata, 5
    Butterscotch and Banana Pudding, 134
    Colorado Game Meatloaf, 98
    Crème Brûlée French Toast, 8
    Dutch Apple Pancake, *9*
    Espresso Ice Cream Cakes, 142-143
    Frisée Salmon Salad, 52
    Ham and Portobello Mushroom Casserole, 12
    Eggplant Croutons, 56-57
    North Fork Rabbit Hash with Poached Eggs, 15
    Portobello and Sage Bread Pudding, 62
    Sausage and Egg Casserole, 20
    Southwest Green Chile Toast, 21
    Spaghetti Squash Fritters, *66*, *67*
    Stracciatella, 88
    Swiss Chard and Gruyère Quiche, 22
elk
    Elk Chops, 101-102
elk, ground
    Colorado Game Meatloaf, 98
Elk Chops with Blackberry Sauce and Garlic
    Mashers, 101-102
endive
    Frisée Salmon Salad, 52
Espresso Ice Cream Cakes with White Chocolate-
    Blueberry Crust, 142-143
espresso powder
    Espresso Ice Cream Cakes, 142-143
    Espresso-Rubbed Beef Tenderloin, 103
Espresso-Rubbed Beef Tenderloin, 103

F

falafel
 Sweet Potato Falafel with Lemon-Tahini Yogurt, 43
farro
 Farro and Barley "Risotto," *45, 50*
Farro and Barley "Risotto," *45, 50*
fennel
 Fennel Gratin, 117–118
 Celeriac, Apple, and Fennel Salad, 40
 Tomato and Watermelon Salad with Fennel Granita, 71
fish, smoked
 Bear Creek Smoked Trout Pâté, 25
flours, xix
Fondue, 104
Fort's™ Famous Black Beans, The, 51
French toast
 Blueberry French Toast Strata, 5
 Crème Brûlée French Toast, 8
Frico Caldo, 31
Frisée Salmon Salad, 52
fritters
 Spaghetti Squash Fritters, *66, 67*
frostings, 135, 136–137, 146
fruit, dried
 Granola, 11
Fruition Farms Ricotta Cheesecake, *x,* 144
Fudge Brownies, 145

G

garlic
 Ajax Baked Chèvre, 24
 Cream of Cilantro Soup, 80
 Garlic and Sage-Stuffed Chicken Breasts, 105
 Tarragon-Garlic Sauce, 120
 roasting, xix
Garlic and Sage-Stuffed Chicken Breasts, 105
ginger
 Gingered Peas, 53
 Gingery Cauliflower Soup, 82
 Mint and Tomato-Ginger Chutney, 109
Gingered Peas, 53
Gingery Cauliflower Soup, 82
gnocchi
 Crisp Gnocchi Salad, 48
Goat Cheese Rosemary Biscuits, *32, 33*
granita, 71
Granola, 11
granola
 Elk Chops, 101–102
 Granola, 11
gratin, 117–118
Green Chile Posole, 83
Green Gazpacho, 84, *85*
greens
 North Fork Rabbit Hash with Poached Eggs, 15
Grilled Palisade Peaches, Serrano Ham, and Rocket Salad, *54, 55*
Grilled Shrimp with Tequila-Orange Sauce and Crispy
 Chorizo-Corn Relish, 106–107
grits
 Stone-Ground Bleu Cheese Grits, 68
Guacamole, 34

H

ham
 Fort's™ Famous Black Beans, The, 51
 Grilled Palisade Peaches, Serrano Ham,
  and Rocket Salad, *54, 55*
 Ham and Portobello Mushroom Casserole, 12
Ham and Portobello Mushroom Casserole, 12
hash
 North Fork Rabbit Hash with Poached Eggs, 15
Heirloom Tomato Salad with Fruition Farms Ricotta, Eggplant
 Croutons, Arugula, and Romesco Vinaigrette, 56–57
Herbed Spaetzle with Mushrooms and Braised Buffalo, 35–36
herbs, xviii
hominy
 Green Chile Posole, 83
 Crispy Chorizo-Corn Relish, 107
honeydew
 Melon Ambrosia, 14

I

ice cream
 Espresso Ice Cream Cakes, 142–143
 Roasted Colorado Peach-Pistachio Brioche Pudding
  with Ice Cream, 150–151

J

Jaeger Schnitzel with Wild Mushroom Sauce, 108

L

lamb
 Colorado Leg of Lamb, 99–100
 Roast Colorado Lamb Chops, 120
 Spicy Malted Lamb Ribs, 41–42
 Whiskey-Braised Lamb Shoulder, 131
lamb, ground
 Colorado Game Meatloaf, 98
 Lamb Slider, 109
 Spaghetti with Braised Lamb Sugo, 127
Lamb Slider with Mint and Tomato-Ginger Chutney, 109
lamb stock
 Whiskey-Braised Lamb Shoulder, 131
leeks
 Chicken Stuffed with Mushrooms, Leeks, and Pistachios, 94
 Cream of Cilantro Soup, 80
Lemon and Asparagus Risotto, 58
Lemon Poppy Seed Bread, 13
lentils
 Lentil Soup with Prosciutto Chips, 86
Lentil Soup with Prosciutto Chips, 86
lettuce
 Baby Spinach and Bibb Lettuce Salad, 46
 Crisp Gnocchi Salad with Wild Mushrooms and Asparagus, 48
 Prosciutto-Wrapped Scallops, 117–118
 Santa Fe Chicken Salad, 64
 Wedge Salad with Saison-Ranch Dressing, 74
lobster
 Lobster Mac and Cheese, 110, *111*
Lobster Mac and Cheese, 110, *111*

M

macadamia nuts
> Valrhona Chocolate-Macadamia Nut Cake, 152

mahi-mahi
> Mahi-Mahi Ceviche, 37

Mahi-Mahi Ceviche, 37

Marsala
> Raspberry-Marsala Cake, 133, 149

mayonnaise
> Southwestern Crab Cakes, *124*, 125–126
> Sriracha, 27

meatloaf
> Colorado Game Meatloaf, 98

Melon Ambrosia, 14

melons
> Melon Ambrosia, 14

milk
> Butterscotch and Banana Pudding, 134
> Tagliatelle Pasta with White Bolognese, 129

Milk Stout Cupcakes, 146

Mountain High Mac and Cheese, 112

mousse
> Chocolate-Cherry Mousse, 138, *139*

muffins
> blueberry, 142–143
> Blueberry Cake Muffins, 4
> Eggnog Muffins, 10

Mushroom and Brown Butter Risotto, 59

mushrooms
> Alamosa Striped Bass, 92
> Chicken Stuffed with Mushrooms, Leeks,
>   and Pistachios, 94
> Crisp Gnocchi Salad with Wild Mushrooms
>   and Asparagus, 48
> Ham and Portobello Mushroom Casserole, 12
> Herbed Spaetzle with Mushrooms and Braised Buffalo, 35–36
> Jaeger Schnitzel with Wild Mushroom Sauce, 108
> Mushroom and Brown Butter Risotto, 59
> North Fork Rabbit Hash with Poached Eggs, 15
> Pan-Roasted Colorado Striped Bass with Chanterelle
>   Mushroom Vin Blanc, 114
> Portobello and Sage Bread Pudding, 62
> Portobello Mushroom Burger, *91*, 116

mussels
> Alamosa Striped Bass, 92
> Chipotle-Steeped Mussels, *23*, 30

N

nectarines
> Plum-Nectarine Crumble, *xi*, 148

New York Strip Steaks with Gonzales Sauce, 113

North Fork Rabbit Hash with Poached Eggs, 15

nuts
> Granola, 11
> Oatmeal Nut Waffles, *16*, 17
> Peach Bread, 19
> toasting, xx

O

Oatmeal Nut Waffles, *16*, 17

oats
> Blueberry Cake Muffins, 4
> Granola, 11
> Oatmeal Nut Waffles, *16*, 17

oils, xviii

Olathe Sweet Corn Spoon Bread, 60

olives
> Ajax Baked Chèvre, 24
> Artichoke, Tomato, and Olive Tapenade, 121

onions
> Cream of Cilantro Soup, 80
> Guacamole, 34
> Tequila-Lime Salsa, 44

Orange, Cranberry, and Walnut Scones, *1*, 18

P

pancakes
> Cowboy Corn Cakes, 6, *7*
> Dutch Apple Pancake, 9

pancetta
> Broiled Pancetta-Wrapped Dates Stuffed with Gorgonzola, 26

Pan-Fried Polenta with Grilled Pears and Gorgonzola Sauce, 38

Pan-Roasted Colorado Striped Bass with Chanterelle Mushroom
   Vin Blanc, 114

pasta
> Chile Crab Rolls with Charred Corn and Sriracha Mayo, 27
> Lobster Mac and Cheese, 110, *111*
> Mountain High Mac and Cheese, 112
> Spaghetti with Braised Lamb Sugo, 127
> Tagliatelle Pasta with White Bolognese, 129

pâté
> Bear Creek Smoked Trout Pâté, 25

Peach BBQ Pork Spareribs, 115

Peach Bread, 19

peaches
> Grilled Palisade Peaches, Serrano Ham,
>   and Rocket Salad, *54*, 55
> Peach BBQ Pork Spareribs, 115
> Peach Bread, 19
> Roasted Colorado Peach-Pistachio Brioche Pudding, 150–151

pears
> Pan-Fried Polenta with Grilled Pears and Gorgonzola Sauce, 38
> Pear Tart, *xx*, 147

Pear Tart, *xx*, 147

peas
> Fondue, 104
> Gingered Peas, 53

peppers, bell
> Fort's™ Famous Black Beans, The, 51
> Heirloom Tomato Salad, 56–57
> Quinoa, Black Bean, and Corn Pilaf, 63
> Roast Colorado Lamb Chops, 120
> roasting, xx
> Red Pepper-Citrus Sauce, 122–123
> Southwestern Crab Cakes, *124*, 125–126
> Tequila-Lime Salsa, 44
> *See also* chiles; chipotle

pheasant
> Smoked Pheasant Soup, 87

pie crusts, xi, xx, 147, 148